OPTICAL FIBER AND SOLITONS

OPTICAL FIBER AND SOLITONS

By

Dr. K. Sonamuthu

Reader

Deptt. of Physics

J.N.R. Mahavidyalaya

Port Blair

Andaman & Nicobar

DISCOVERY PUBLISHING HOUSE PVT. LTD.

NEW DELHI-110 002

Published by:
Tilak Wasan
DISCOVERY PUBLISHING HOUSE PVT. LTD.
4383/4B, Ansari Road, Darya Ganj
New Delhi-110 002 (India)
Phone : +91-11-23279245, 43596064-65
Fax : +91-11-23253475
E-mail : discoverypublishinghouse@gmail.com
sales@discoverypublishinggroup.com
web : www.discoverypublishinggroup.com

***First Edition:* 2011**
***Reprinted:* 2016**

ISBN: 978-81-8356-913-2

Optical Fiber and Solitons

Printed at:
Infinity Imaging Systems
Delhi

Preface

This book is titled with *'Optical Fiber and Solitons'* consist of five units. The first unit deals with that apart from optical fiber, an optical transmission system would need, in a practical system, two other key elements, namely, the transmitter and receiver which had been already developed independently.

In order to send a light signal through optical fiber, it is required to have a source that emits a bright directional signal. Also, since light signals are often in digital form (that is, the information is conveyed in the form of series of light pulses), the light sources should be capable of being turned on and off quickly. The more rapid the modulation, the more would be the information conveyed in a given time.

Basically, fiber optic transmission arose from a synthesis of two hitherto unrelated technologies: the semiconductor technology and the optical waveguide technology. The former technology would supply the raw materials for the light sources and detectors needed in an optical transmission system, while the second technology would give rise to a transmission medium optical fiber. In the late 1960's it was realized that a combination of the two technologies would lead to a transmission system that would have certain inherent advantages over conventional copper systems, especially in the case of the digital systems of the developing countries. Apart from having lower transmission losses than copper, the fiber provides higher bandwidth. These two basic advantages would give systems with longer repeater spacing and higher information carrying capacities than are possible with copper.

Various processes are being modified such as perform making, melting process, melting environment, homogenization/fining, and reactive atmosphere processing. The performance of optical fibers, specifically the transmission losses, bandwidth and strength, is strongly influenced by the fiber drawing and coating process.

Finally this chapter ends with advantages of optical fiber describing that, in addition to the advantages of having extra information bandwidth using light as carrier signal, the optical fiber communication systems have several other advantages over the conventional systems and with the advent of the first generation fiber transmission systems in the market, fiber research and development would continue. The progress, achieved in fiber research and development have been achieved by people, with highly specialized skills, who have used innovative but costly equipment to produce a limited variety of experimental fiber samples.

The second chapter deals with dispersion in optical fibers and the importance of dispersion of optical signals through fibers. The attenuation or transmission loss in an optical fiber is the most important factors widely used in the study of fiber communications. An advantage of the optical fiber as a telecommunications medium is the small size of the fiber itself. With a typical diameter of only 125 microns, it possess a large variety of properties. The fiber design utilizes the fact that electromagnetic waves, in a dielectric, tend to travel in a region of high refractive index called the 'core'. The perform is fabricated by means of modified chemical vapour deposition (MCVD) process. Initially the substrate tube is cleaned by hydrofluoric acid and fire-polished to remove stress in the glass and later on etched with freon to remove surface impurities. The glass used in optical fiber is not a crystalline solid but an amorphous one. It is prepared by allowing glass to cool from the molten state at high temperatures until it freezes. When it is still plastic, glass is drawn out in tension into its fiber form. During the forming process following two defects may arise.

There are three mechanisms that contribute to the absorption losses. These are: (1) Ultraviolet absorption; (2) Infra-red absorption; and (3) Ion resonance absorption.

This chapter ends with the combination of losses in fibers such as Rayleigh Scattering losses, material absorption losses.

The chapter third deals with effect of dispersion on pulse transmission. Several dispersion effects are encountered by the pulse of light propagating through a fiber and these act to spread out the pulse in the time domain changing the shape of the pulse. When a pulse of light is transmitted in a fiber, it will be propagated over several different paths corresponding to the excited modes and come out of the far end at slightly different times. The refractive index of core glass of fiber is not the same for lights of different wavelengths but it depends on the wavelength of light in a complicated way. When a pulse of light transmitted contains components of several wavelengths centered about a center wavelength. When a fiber could be so operated that the multipath and material dispersions are all eliminated as should be the case for a single mode fiber operation near λ=1.3μm, then a third dispersion mechanism will predominate except in the case ideally monochromatic light. Unfortunately ideal monochromatic courses are not available so that the light transmitted consists of component of several wavelengths near the central wavelength λ_0.

This chapter ends with total dispersion in a single mode fiber. In order to minimize the total dispersion of a signal through a single mode fiber, it is essential to operate it to a wavelength longer than 1.37μm. At that wavelength the small value of material dispersion cancels the small wave guide dispersion.

The fourth chapter deals with optimization of dispersion in optical fiber using solitons through the non-linear schrodinger equation and it describes that Optical fibers have created a revolution in the field of telecommunication and have become the backbone of today's global communication networks. Optical fiber communication is considered to be more advantageous because, it has large channel handling capacity, high signal to noise ratio due to presence of low noise, no electromagnetic interference etc. In this analysis, it has been rather provided excessive effective amplification in the DDF so that the input sinusoidal signal could evolve into higher order soliton. The term 'soliton" was introduced in the 1960's, but the scientific research of solitons had started in the 19th century when John Scott-Russell observed a large solitary wave in a canal near Edinburgh. In the days of Scott Russell, there was much debate concerning the very existence of this kind of solitary waves. Now-a-days, many model equations of non-linear phenomena are known to possess soliton solutions. This chromatic-dispersion phenomenon substantially consists of a widening in the duration of the pulses forming the signal during their travel through the fiber. This widening is due to the fact that the different chromatic components of each pulse are characterized each by its own wavelength and travel in the fiber at different speeds. The system model of the proposed idea and the pulse shapes at each stage for the precise analysis of pulse propagation, the non-linear Schrodinger equation [NSE] was solved numerically using variation approach. It has been shown that the soliton in fiber links employing compensating fiber with variable dispersion based on the variational approach for the solution of the non-schrodinger equation (NSE) by using simple system criterion.

This chapter ends with optimization of dispersion which says that the dispersion compensation scheme is reported where the uniform DCF is replaced by fiber with decreasing and increasing dispersion profiles.

Finaly, the fifth chapter deals with the applications of Soliton for the feature Network. We have presented a comprehensive overview of the recent theoretical results on the physics of the ring-profile optical solitary waves and soliton clusters carrying a finite angular momentum. Depending on the value of the total angular momentum and the cluster structure, such solitarywaves either fragment quickly into several fundamental solitons that fly off the ring, or propagate stably for many diffraction lengths with rotating intensity and phase. We have demonstrated a link between different types of ring-profile self-trapped state, such as vortex solitons, necklace beams and ring-like soliton clusters. We have also discussed the beam stabilization by incoherent coupling of several beam components, and have demonstrated the existence of novel types of ring-profile vector soliton with rotating intensity and phase. Many of these structures belong to the class of self-trapped optical beams and, therefore, they are possible only in a self-focussing optical medium. Such structures provide a non-trivial generalization to the optical vortices and phase-front dislocations, associated with the field angular momentum and spiralling optical beams.

Further this chapter deals with the Soliton based optical fiber communication systems, using EDFA's,are more suitable for long haul communication because of their very high information carrying capacity and repeater less transmission. These systems are still to be developed for field applications. When transmission demand will increase and device technology will improve, they will be certainly employed in field. By using soliton based optical switches multi GBPS data rate can be achieved for optical computation also.

Today the replacement of electronic repeaters which required the subsequent previous optical electronic and ulterior electronic-optical transformations by optical Erbium Doped Fiber Amplifiers (EDFA) fed through laser diodes, as providing a fully optical point-to-point link through which any bit stream can be transmitted regardless of its data format, velocity or carrier wavelength, has added versatility to the system which in addition results more reliable due to the reduction in components. That further allows with traditional NRZ format, dispersion-shifted fibers and other techniques designed to compensate for dispersion, to increase the channel capacity in commercial optical links up to about 1 0 ~ b pasn d 10.000 km of repeaterless distance. With the use of EDFAs, multiplication of the channel capacity through the use of several carrier wavelengths, the so-called Wavelength Division Multiplexing (WDM) technique, is economically feasible. As allowing accumulation of non-linear effects along the link, EDFAs further open the door to *soliton* based transmission. Concerning fiber transmission, optical solitons designate these pulses arising from an interplay between linear dispersion and the non-linearity present in the fibre which due to its very special properties can propagate over very large distances without significant alteration of its temporal profile. One may say that when solitonic propagation takes place the linear dispersion is compensated through the non-linearity.

Authors

Contents

1

FABRICATION OF SILICON-BASED GLASS FIBERS FOR OPTICAL COMMUNICATION

Introduction

Optical communication systems date back two centuries, to the 'optical telegraph' that French engineer Claude Chappe invented in the 1790s. His system was a series of semaphores mounted on towers, where human operators relayed messages from one tower to the next. It beat hand-carried messages shads down, but by the mid-19th century it was replaced by the electric telegraph, leaving a scattering of 'Telegraph Hills' as its most visible legacy.

Alexander Graham Bell patented an optical telephone system, which he called the Photophone, in 1880, but his earlier invention the telephone, proved for more practical. He dreamed of sending signals through the air, but the atmosphere didn't transmit light as reliably as wires carried electricity. In the decades that followed, light was used for a few special applications.

In the intervening years, a new technology slowly took root that would ultimately solve the problem of optical transmission, although it was a long time before it was adapted for communications. It depended on the phenomenon of total internal reflection, which can confine light in a material surrounded by other materials with lower refractive index, such as glass in air. In the 1840s, Swiss physicist Daniel Collodon and French physicist Jacques Babinet showed that light could be guided along jets of water for fountain displays. British physicist John Tyndall popularized light guiding in a demonstration he first used in 1854, guiding light in a jet of water flowing from a tank. By the turn of the century, inventors realized that bent quartz rods could carry light, and patented them as dental illuminators. By the 1940s, many doctors used illuminated plexiglass tongue depressors.

Optical fibers went a step further. They are essentially transparent rods of glass or plastic stretched so they are long and flexible. During the 1920s, John Logie Baird in England and Clarence W.Hansell in the United States patented the idea of using arrays of hollow pipes or transparent rods to transmit images for television or facsimile systems. However, the first person known to have demonstrated image transmission though a bundle of optical fibers was Heinrich Lamm, than a medical student in Munich. His goal was to look inside inaccessible parts of the body, and in a 1930 paper the reported transmitting the image of a light bulb filament through a short bundle. However, the unclad fibers transmitted images poorly, and the rise of the Nazis forced Lamm, a Jew, to move to America and abandon his dreams of becoming professor of medicine.

Neither Van Heel nor Hopkins and Kapany made bundles that could carry light far, their reports the fiber optics revolution. The crucial innovation was made by van Heel, stimulated by a conversation with the American optical physicist Brain O'Brien. All earlier fibers were 'bare', with total internal reflection at a glass-air interface. This protected the total reflection surface from contamination, and greatly reduced cross talk between fibers. The next key step was development of glass-clad fibers, by Lawrence Curtiss, then an undergraduate at the University of Machigan working part-time on a project to develop and endoscope to examine the inside of the stomach with physician Basil Hirschowitz, physicist C.Wilbur Peters. By 1960, glass-clad fibers had attenuation of about one decibel per meter, fine for medical imaging, but much too high for communications.

Meanwhile, telecommunications engineers were seeking more transmission bandwidth. Radio and microwave frequencies were in heavy use, so they looked to higher frequencies to carry loads they expected to continue increasing with the growth of television and telephone traffic. Telephone companies though video telephones lurked just around the corner, and would escalate bandwidth demands even further. The cutting edge of communications research were millimeter-wave systems, in which hallow pipes served as waveguides to circumvent poor atmospheric transmission at tens of gigahertz, where wavelengths were in the millimeter range.

Even higher optical frequencies seemed a logical next step in 1958 at Alec Reeves, the forward looking engineer at Britian's Standard Telecommunications Laboratories who invented digital pulse-code modulation before World War-II. Other people climbed on the optical communications bandwagon when the laser was invented in 1960. Optical fibers had attracted some attention because they were analogous in theory to plastic dielectric waveguides used in certain microwave applications. In 1961, Elias Snitzer at American Optical, working with Hicks at Mosaic Fabrictions, demonstrated the similarity by drawing fibers with cores. So they carried light in only one waveguide mode. However virtually everyone considered fibers too lossy for communications; attenuation of a decibel per meter was fine for looking September 1970, they announced they had made single-mode fibers with attenuation at the 633 nanometer helium-neon below 20 dB/km. The fibers were fragile, but tests at the new British Post Office Research Laboratories facility in Martlesham Heath confirmed the low loss.

The Corning breakthrough was among the most dramatic of many developments that opened the door to fiber-optic communications. In the same year, Bell Labs and a team at the Ioffe Physical Institute in Leningrad made the first semiconductor diode lasers able to emit continuous wave at room temperature. Over the next several years, fiber losses dropped dramatically, aided both by improved fabrication methods and by the shift to longer wavelengths where fibers have inherently lower attenuation[1,2].

Genesis of Fiber Optics

A light source a light guide and a light detector constitute the principal elements of a fiber optic transmission system. The light source receives a coded electrical signal (such a voice, data or video information) transforms it into a light signal, and steers this signal on to the light guide. The light signal is confined along the light guide for transmission to the detector, where it is received and reconverted into the original electrical message. Although this concept is simple, it emerged only within the last fifteen years.

The visible portion of the electromagnetic spectrum, namely light, has been used for centuries, as in the case of hilltop beacons, smoke signals (reflected light) and even Alexander Graham Bell's 1980 photo phone, which was nothing but a device that modulated the incoming sunlight and reflected it over several hundred meters for detection and demodulation back into speech.

The limitations of such line-of-sight communication systems lies in the fact that the light signal is unguided; instead it would be transmitted through the atmosphere, encountering distortion problems, even when weather positions are fair. Such signals can be scatted or blocked entirely by physical obstacles; also, in the case of messages which are confidential, the signal can be intercepted and even deciphered with a knowledge of the code used. So a viable light-wave communication system needs a light guide so as to preserve the signal and hence increase the reliability and distance of signal transmission.

Development of a Light Guide

Even though the possibility of guiding light had been demonstrated as early as in 1854, in the form of reflections in a curved stream of water coming out of a hole in the side of a pail, the concept of a practical light and viable guide emerged only in 1910 in the form of a solid cylinder capable of guiding a wide range of electromagnetic waves, including those of visible light. Another possible light guide emerged in the form of a hollow tube with a highly reflective metal coating on its inner surface. In either case light injected into one end of the guide, bounded back and forth; the high signal loss, of these devices, occurring when light had to pass through curved paths to change direction, rendered such devices impractical. Another device was in the form of a heated gas-filled conduit; but it was also not suitable for commercial applications on account of its disadvantages of complexity and high cost.

In the 1930s experiments were conducted on a guide comprising simple filaments of glass fiber packed into bundles. In a time span of twenty years, these glass fiber bundles were being used as light conduits for card readers; later they were used in medical endoscopes. At this time, optical fibers also began to appear in photography where, fused together, the glass fiber bundles were used as face plates in image intensifiers and field flatteners. Each fiber had become a composite structure. The core region, with its high refractive index, carried most of the light and was surrounded by a cladding that had a lower refractive index. Although this design improved the transmission efficiency as well as the handling capacity of each fiber, and also reduced the cross talk amongst the fibers in a bundle, signal losses restricted the optical fiber to applications of utmost a few meters.

By 1970, leading American glass manufactures were able to produce fiber, of sufficient purity, for use in the telecommunication industry with an attenuation of less than 20 dB/km. The fiber was fabricated by using a method of synthesizing silica glass. The raw materials were vapourized and deposited inside a length of quartz glass tubing, which was then solidified into a rod and drawn in the form of a fiber.

Transmitter and Receiver Elements

Apart from optical fiber, an optical transmission system would need, in a practical system, two other key elements, namely, the transmitter and receiver which had been already developed independently.

In order to send a light signal through optical fiber, it is required to have a source that emits a bright directional signal. Also, since light signals are often in digital form (that is, the information is conveyed in the form of series of light pulses), the light sources should be capable of being turned on and off quickly. The more rapid the modulation, the more would be the information conveyed in a given time.

By 1970, the different technologies, underlying the complete fiber optic transmission system, had coalesced. The following decade saw research institutions as well as manufactures of telecommunications equipment seriously engaged in efforts to refine the components and assemble them into practical optical transmission systems.

With the potentiality of the glass fiber was unlimited information carrying capacities at certain wavelengths, the Bell Laboratories developed a laser with a promise of continuous operation at room temperature for more than a thousand hours. Other phenomenal developments followed, including the fabrication of a commercial optical cable, a reliable high power LED as well as prototype splice and connector, a fiber optic avalanche photo-diode detector and a fiber link installed on a destroyed. By 1978, the Japanese had succeeded in reducing fiber losses to a low figure of 0.2 dB/km. At the same time several fiber systems were being processed and undergoing field testing, so as to be used in telephone systems. Currently, hundreds of fiber optic transmission systems, of experimental and operational types, are in use around the world.

Fiber Optics Transmission Systems

While radio and copper wire transmission systems have been in vogue for a long time, light wave communication has sparked renewed interest all over the world by different telecommuni-cation organizations. This time the transmission medium is not air (which is a poor light conductor) but cables optical fibers. In the last twelve years, the fiber optics technology has advanced to the point where practical fiber systems present viable alternatives to copper in telecommunications.

Basically, fiber optic transmission arose from a synthesis of two hitherto unrelated technologies: the semiconductor technology and the optical waveguide technology. The former technology would supply the raw materials for the light sources and detectors needed in an optical transmission system, while the second technology would give rise to a transmission medium optical fiber. In the late 1960's it was realized that a combination of the two technologies would lead to a transmission system that would have certain inherent advantages over conventional copper systems, especially in the case of the digital systems of the developing countries.

Apart from having lower transmission losses than copper, the fiber provides higher bandwidth. These two basic advantages would give systems with longer repeater spacing and higher information carrying capacities than are possible with copper. The smaller size and lower weight of fiber help to make cables that are easier to be handled and installed; in addition, the fibers themselves enjoy immunity to electromagnetic interference such as lightening, ac induction, and cross talk from other fibers in a cable. The most attractive feature of the fiber lies in the availability of abundant and inexpensive silica material used to make the fiber for use in attractive transmission systems of low cost.

Fiber in Telecommunication Systems

Communication, between switching office, is normally via the trunk facilities. Trunk transmission in the network has been primarily of the analogue type until 1962 when the DSI rate

(1.544 Mb/s) of digital transmission was introduced. Since then the DSI rate copper systems have multiplied and are now the standard carrier systems, especially in 10 km-320 km trucking applications. The success of these systems was due to their better performance and less cost as compared to the systems they replaced. In this context, fiber optic systems would be very competitive and viable among the next generation trunk transmission systems.

Optical Fiber in Short Distance Communication

Numerous techniques[3,4,5] are developed for fabrication of glass fibers so as to get better optical properties suitable for optical communication, and also to combat with ever increasing demand of fiber in diverse application areas. Various processes are being modified such as perform making, melting process, melting environment, homogenization/fining, and reactive atmosphere processing[6]. Hermetic carbon coating has been shown to be effective barrier for water and hydrogen.[7,8,9] Polymers such as ultra violet radiation curable acrylate and Teflon-FEP are used as coating for fluoride glass optical fibers.[10] However, these materials have high permeability of water and hence are not adequate for fabrication of high strength optical fibers. Oxide glass has low permeability of water than fluoride glass. Efforts are also made to fabricate plastic optical fibers as a compliment for glass fibers in short distance communication links.[11] The fabrication and characterization of side hole single mode optical fibers have been situated.[12] The thermal modelling is reported for optical fibers drawing process to see that effect of fiber diameter and drawing speed on temperature distribution.[13] The most fundamental physical parameter for optical fiber is geometry, since the dimension of the fiber determines its ability to splice and to be terminated. Therefore, when the fiber is fabricated, it is important to study the above mentioned parameters, which are useful in assessing the communication performance of the fiber.

Fiber Fabrication

At first it seemed that this low-loss transmission requirement would be very difficult to achieve, but finally tremendous advances have been made in several laboratories. The Southampton University held the world record for the best fiber, with a loss of only 5.8 dB/km, in a configuration consisting of a fine glass capillary tube as the cladding filled with a special liquid (hexachlorobutadiene) as the core. Other laboratories in the USA improved on this result using solid fibers consisting of silica doped with titania, germania or boric oxide as one component and pure silica as the other. Again, the Southampton University produced another new type of fiber using a rather unexpected material namely phospho-silicate glass.

Preform Fabrication

Optically transparent oxide glasses fall into two main types: multi-component glasses and high silica content glasses. The fabrication processes, for these glasses, are different, since high silica glasses require a higher fabrication temperature than multi-component glasses; glass objects are made of multi-component type. The attenuation and dispersion, of multi-component glass and of plastic fibers, are too high to be practical for most telecommunication applications.

Fiber Drawing

The performance of optical fibers, specifically the transmission losses, bandwidth and strength, is strongly influenced by the fiber drawing and coating process. This process must be treated as an integrated operation designed to impart desired properties to the resulting fiber which consists of feed glass, heat source, fiber diameter monitor, cooling system, coating applicator, curing apparatus, and fiber puller/winding mechanism. The components are arranged in vertical position to take advantage of gravitational forces. The feed glass perform is fed at speed of 0.02 – 0.03 cm/s depending on the heat source, perform diameter and draw speed. Continuous lengths of more than 40-km have been drawn from such a perform in one drawing. Fiber drawing proceeds by heating the tip of the perform to a molten state and allowing it to extend under the force of gravity downward into a fine-diameter filament whereas pulling and winding mechanism sustains force. The fiber diameter is monitored continuously as the fiber passes through the furnace. Any variation of the fiber diameter is detected by a control device that automatically readjusts the temperature and the speed of pulling mechanism to compensate for initial change. Since this bare fiber consists of core and clad, the fiber diameter is an important parameter, which influences wave propagation phenomenon used in optical fiber. When the fiber comes out of the furnace, it is cooled in the presence of helium gas without altering its physical dimension. Then it enters the coating applicator immediately as shown in fig. 1.1

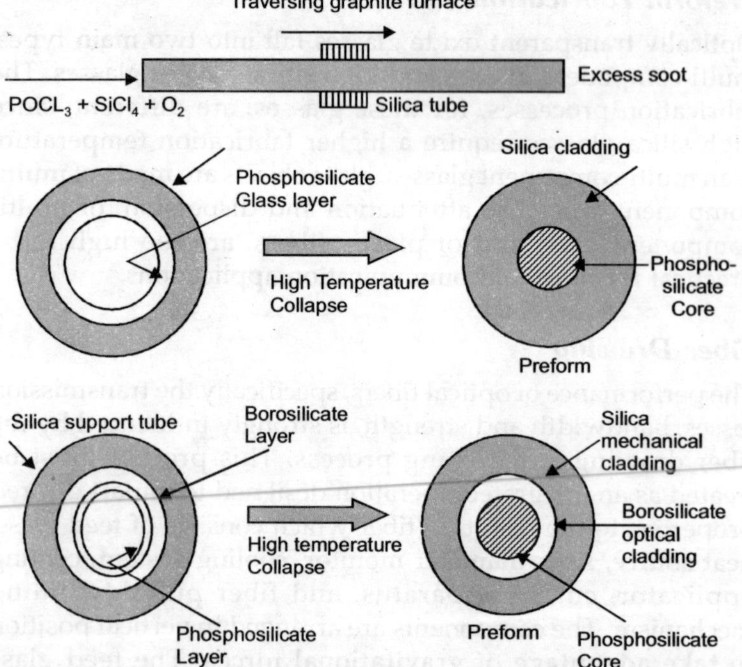

Fig. 1.1 : Two-layer process of manufacture of phosphosilicate fibers, with silica tube acting as a supporting structure.

Fiber Optics Technology

Light Through Fibers

Let us consider a construction Fig.1.2 with n_1 and n_2 being refractive indices of two materials, i.e. the core and cladding surrounded by air of refractive index n. Also let us

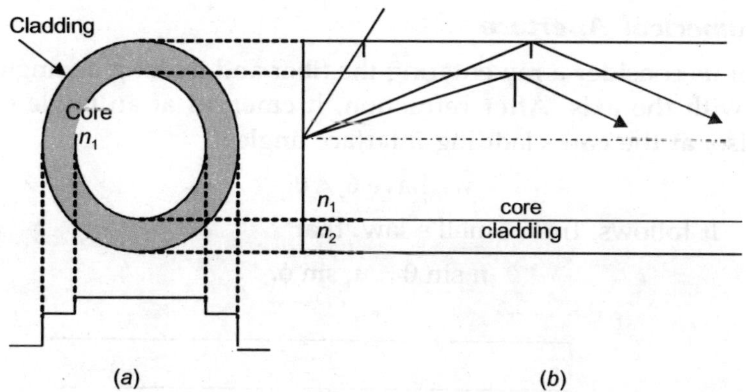

Fig. 1.2 : Propagation of light through fibers

Assuming that $n_1 > n_2$. In the case of ray 1, the incident ray strikes the core and cladding interface at an angle $\theta_i > \theta_c$ (critical angle) and is totally internally reflected in the core. Ray 2 strikes the interface at an angle $\theta_i < \theta_c$ and is refracted into the cladding. But it again strikes the cladding-to-air surface $\theta_i > \theta_c$ here θ_c is the critical angle for cladding-to-air surface. This ray will reflect back into the cladding, then to the core and so on.

In the case of ray 3, $\theta_i < \theta_c$ and $\theta_i < \theta_c$; the ray is from the core to the cladding and to the air.

Ray 1 is the most important ray from fiber-optics points of view. However, ray 2 also propagates through the length of such a construction, but scattering and absorption are very high in the irregular cladding material so as to result in high loss as compared to the one through the core. Since some of the energy will always travel through the material outside the cores, cladding is provided instead of air surrounding the core. However, the main effort of the designer will be to trap the energy in the core to the maximum extent. This type of construction of the fiber is known as step-index fiber, in the case refractive indices, of the materials, would vary in discrete steps n_1 and n_2.

Numerical Aperture

Let us consider a ray entering the fiber and making an angle θ with the axis. After refraction, it emerges at an angle ϕ. Also, at the core-cladding interface angle,

we have $\theta_i < \theta_c$

It follows, from Smell's law, that

$$n \sin \theta = n_1 \sin \phi.$$

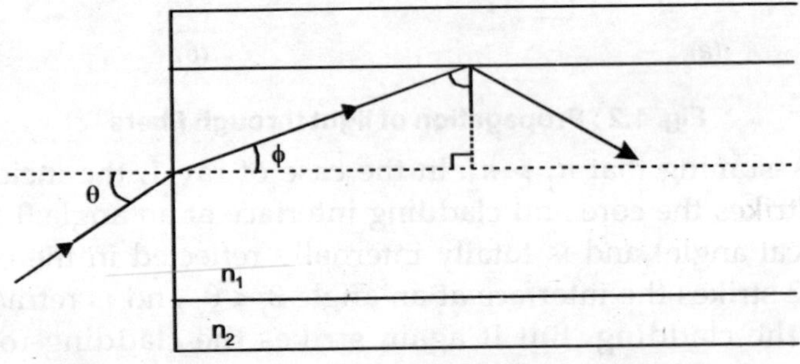

Fig. 1.3 : Refraction of light through fiber

But $\quad n_1 \sin \phi = n_1 \sin (90 - \theta_i) = n_1 \cos \theta_i$

So that $\quad n \sin \theta = n_1 \cos \theta_c$

When $\quad \theta_i = \theta_c$

$$n \sin \theta = n_1 \cos \theta,$$

But we know that

$$\sin \theta_c = \frac{n_2}{n_1}$$

So that $\quad \cos \theta_c = \dfrac{n_1^2 - n_2^2}{n_1^2}$

Hence $n \sin \theta = n_1, \frac{n_1^2 - n_2^2}{n_1}$ = Numerical Aperture of the fiber.

With $n = 1$ (for air)

We have N.A. = $\sin \theta = (n_1^2 - n_2^2) = \theta$ (for small angles)

In order to have $\theta_I > \theta_c$ (for total internal reflection), ϕ or (in turn) θ must be small.

The quantity, N.A. = $\sin \theta = (n_1^2 - n_2^2)$, defines the maximum acceptable light cone for a fiber of the given refractive index; this quantity is a very important parameter of the fiber.

Multimode and Monomode Fibers

When the core diameter, of the fiber (Fig. 1.4), is large,

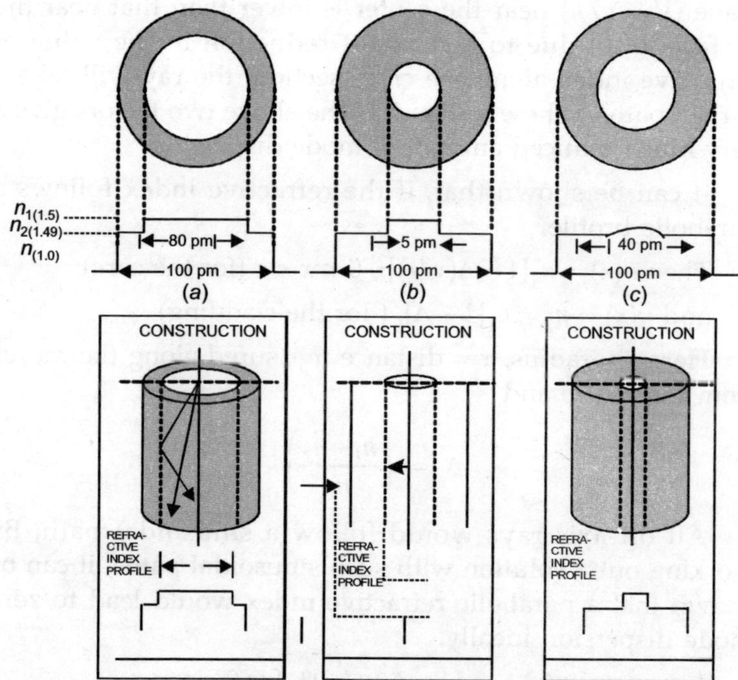

Fig. 1.4 : Multimode propagation in fibers

multimode propagation is possible; under such conditions; a fiber is referred to as to multimode fiber. The disadvantage of such a fiber would be its wide dispersion. With the dependence of dispersion on a, it is possible to reduce the dispersion of the fiber, if its diameter is reduced to an extent that a single mode can be propagated; in that case, this type of fiber would be known as a *mono-mode fiber*.

Grade Index Fiber

Another solution, to the problem of mode or multi-path dispersion is obtained by a graded-index fiber whose refractive index is not constant along the radius of the core but varies according to a certain present relation from the core centre towards the outer diameter, such as the core index decreasing along the radius from the center. Since the core center has a higher refractive index, the velocity of the light wave ($V = c/n$) near the center is lower than that near the surface; also, due to a constant reduction in the value of refractive index along the cross-section, the ray will take a curved path as show in Fig. 1.4. The above two factors give a very much reduced amount of mode dispersion.

It can be shown that, if the refractive index follows a parabolic profile,

Then $n(x) = n_1[1 - \Delta(x/r)]^2$, $0 < x < r$ (for the core)

and $n(x) = n_2 = n_1[1 - \Delta]$, (for the cladding)

Here r = radius, x = distance measured along the radius from the centre and

$$\Delta = \left(\frac{n_1 - n_2}{n_1}\right)$$

All off-axis rays would follow a sinusoidal path. By working out a solution with such sinusoidal paths, it can be shown that a parabolic refractive index would lead to zero mode dispersion ideally.

In general $n(x) = n_1[1 - \Delta\,(x/r)]^{\alpha}$, for $0 < x < r$

and $n(x) = n_2 = n_1(1 - \Delta)]$ for $x > r$

if $\alpha = \infty$

then $n(x) = n_1$, for $0 < x < r$

and $n(x) = n_2 = n(1 - \Delta)]$ for $x > r$

This applies to a step-index fiber.

This optimum value of α in practice depends upon the materials used for the fiber; this α factor is very important to be controlled during the manufacture of the fiber.

The very small difference, between n_1 and n_2 implies that the axis angle, for a core-trapped ray, is small. Such fibers are referred to as weakly guided structures. The multimode step index fiber is useful for only short transmission lengths because of its large dispersion, but provides a higher coupling efficiency due to its large core cross-section. The mono-mode fiber, on the other hand, overcomes the problem of multi-path dispersion, but has the disadvantage of a very small cross-sectional area. The graded–index fiber, however, exhibits relatively loss-mode dispersion, with a relatively large core area.

Advantages of Optical Fibers

In addition to the advantages of having extra information bandwidth using light as carrier signal, the optical fiber communication systems have several other advantages over the conventional systems.

They are as follows :

(*i*) By virtue of its manufacturing material, it is very light and easy to handle;

(*ii*) Because of very low transmission loss, the distance between repeater stations increased greatly;

(*iii*) Optical fibers can be used in explosive as well as high voltage environment due to the absence of any hazards arising out of short circuits;

(*iv*) It is ideal for secret communication systems because it is very difficult to tap but very easy to monitor;

(*v*) They are virtually unaffected by outdoor atmospheric conditions;

(*vi*) Since the only carrier in the fiber is light, there is no possibility of a;

(*vii*) spark from a broken fiber;

(*viii*) It will not corrode and is unaffected by mot chemicals. It can be buried directly in most kinds of solids or exposed to most corrosive atmospheres in chemical plants;

(*ix*) They are immune to electromagnetic interference and avoid cross talk.

Future for Fiber Optics

With the advent of the first generation fiber transmission systems in the market, fiber research and development would continue. The progress, achieved in fiber research and development have been achieved by people, with highly specialized skills, who have used innovative but costly equipment to produce a limited variety of experimental fiber samples. Manufacturing, however, requires a large volume production at minimal cost. Much room for innovative engineering development lies in the translation of technology into an industrial product.

Continuous research is being directed towards bringing the fiber attenuation level over a broad range of wavelengths close to the theoretical limit, which, at the 1550-nm wavelength, is about 0.2 dB/km. The commercial production of these low loss fibers should be possible in the near future. The loss level of these fibers can improve only slightly, since hydroxyl water has already been almost totally eliminated. Heavier-atom-halide materials, however, have the potential to raise the molecular absorption of the fiber to the 3000-5000 nm range where Rayleigh scattering and ultraviolet absorption are extremely low. The potential impact of such fibers would be properly estimated after investigating the possibility of manufacture of such fibers and associated compatible light sources, detectors, and splicing techniques. The quest, for higher bandwidths, is straighter forward.

With fibers subjected to very high levels of optical power density, there would be non-linear refractive index effects which may lead to the generation of new lasing wavelengths, wavelengths filtering and pulse compression. Investigations have already been launched to study the importance of such effect as well as fiber sensors for the detection of thermal, acoustic, mechanical and electromagnetic signals. These properties may contribute to future forms of fiber optics for telecommunications.

REFERENCES

1. Fleming JW, 'Fiber Optics Technicians Hand Book' by JIM Hayes, Delmar Publ. New York, Electron Lett. 14, (326), 1978.
2. Jeff Hecht, 'The Story of Fiber Optics', Oxford University Press, New York, 1999.
3. Beals K J., Day CR, Duncan WJ, Dunn AG, Dunn PL, Newns GR and Wright JV, 5th European Conference on Optical Fiber Communication (New York: McGraw Hill), 1979.
4. Izawa T., Sudo S., and Hanawa F., Trans. IEEE 62, (779) 1979.
5. MacChesney JB Proc.IEEE 68(1181), 1980.
6. France Paul, Caster SF Moore W. and Williams JR in 'Optical Fiber Material and Processing', MRS Symp.Proc. 172 (134), 1990.
7. Lumair PJ, Kranz KS, Walker KL and Huff RG Elect. Lett. 24(132),1988.
8. Huff RG, Dimarcello FV and Hast Jr AC, Tech. Digest OFC Paper TUG 2, 1989.
9. Lu K.E., Lee MT Powers D.R. and Glassman S., in Tech. Digest, PDI, OFC (425), 1989.
10. Ihishi V., Fujiura K. and Takahashi S., MRS Symp. Proc, 1990.
11. Izawa T., Shabita N. and Takeda A., Appl. Phys. Lett. 3133, 1977.
12. Izawa T. and Sudo S., 'Optical Fiber Materials and Fabrication' (36), 1987.
13. Papamichel H. and Miaoulis J., MRS Symp. Proc. 172(43), 1990.

2

DISPERSIONS IN OPTICAL FIBER

Introduction

In this chapter some of the important optical properties of fibers are discussed. They are attenuation (loss) and dispersion of an optical signal propagation through fibers.

Attenuation

The attenuation or transmission loss in an optical fiber is the most important factors widely used in the study of fiber communications. The maximum transmission distance prior to the signal restoration is determined by attenuation in the channel and the optical fiber communications became attractive when the transmission loss in a fiber became less than that in a metallic conductor.

Attenuation Units

Signal attenuation or transmission loss is defined as the ratio of the input transmitted optical power P_{in} into a fiber to the out put (received) optical power P_{out} from the fiber. This ratio is a function of the operating wavelength. The symbol α_{dB} is commonly used to express the attenuation in decibels per kilometer.

$$\alpha_{dB} = \frac{1}{L}\left(10\log_{10}\left(\frac{P_{in}}{P_{out}}\right)\right) \qquad ...(2.1)$$

Where L is the length in km of the fiber.

An ideal fiber would have no power loss so that $P_{out} = P_{in}$. This is equivalent to 0 = dB attenuation. An ideal fiber is not found in practice. Suppose for a fiber $\alpha_{dB} = 3$ dB/km is average power loss, and it means that the optical signal power will decrease by 50 per cent over a path length of one kilometer. The numerical values may be obtained using the relationship.

$$\frac{P_{in}}{P_{out}} = 10^{dB/10} \qquad ...(2.2)$$

The basis attenuation mechanisms in a fiber are scattering, absorption and the radiative losses of the optical energy. Absorption is associated with the fiber material and with the structural imperfection in the optical waveguide. Attenuation due to radiative effects originates from both microscopic perturbations of the fiber geometry.

Optical Fiber and Cable

Analytical research, on optical fiber, began in the early 1970's. In 1974, experimental silica fibers were fabricated using a chemical vapour deposition process.

Optical Properties

An advantage of the optical fiber as a telecommunications medium is the small size of the fiber itself. With a typical diameter of only 125 microns, it possess a large variety of properties. The fiber design utilizes the fact that electro-magnetic waves, in a dielectric, tend to travel in a region of high refractive index called the 'core'. In a typical fiber, this core has a graded refractive index is 50 microns in diameter and is surrounded by a cladding a glass of lower index. This cladding, in turn, is protected by a plastic jacket with an outside diameter of 330 microns.

In the currently designed fibers, light rays, that enter the core within a core having a half-angle $\theta - 10^0$ [corresponding to numerical aperture (NA) = sin θ = 0.18], will propagate along the fiber. The larger the numerical aperture the more efficient would be the coupling of light from a source and the better would be the signal transmission around bends. But a large value of NA would be associated with higher attenuation and larger signal distortion.[1]

The initial break-through, that permitted optical fibers to be used for telecommunications, appeared when the signal loss due to the fiber was reduced to less than 20dB per km. This reduction resulted from the technique of holding down metallic and hydroxyl ion impurities in the fiber to a few parts per billion levels and from the ability to manufacture fibers almost totally free of structural imperfections. In the past decade, fiber-induced signal loss has been substantially reduced. So, the most recent generation of fibers can carry telecommunications signals in the wavelength range between 700 nm and 1800 nm. At the wavelengths of 1300 nm and 1550 nm, loss levels, of less than 1 dB/km, have been achieved. Attenuation, at shorter wavelengths, is dominated by Rayleigh scattering, while attenuation, at longer wavelengths, is due to infra-red absorption, the peak around 1400 nm being from hydroxyl absorption. Light transmitters and receivers are currently available for the 840 nm region. Intensive research and development, on transmitters and receivers, would help to exploit the longer wavelength regions, in the fiber, with a loss of less than 1dB/km.

As the amount of attenuation has been reduced over the years, there remains the problem of a second optical property, namely, dispersion. Dispersion causes signal pulse broadening which, in turn, limits the pulse rate or signaling frequency that a fiber can transmit. Two types of dispersion exist: chromatic dispersion and multi-mode dispersion. At a wavelength of about 840 nm, chromatic dispersion causes pulse broadening of about 0.1 ns per kilometer on fiber per nanometer of source width.[2]

Strength

The theoretical tensile strength, of silica-based glass, is estimated to be a high as 7GPs (1 million psi). The theoretical value of strength exceeds the measured value of strength, since fiber is concentrated on the tips of small cracks distributed on the glass surface. These microcracks limit the tensile strength of the fiber. They may be inherent to the material, arising from impurities or defects in its chemical structure. Alternatively, they may develop during the process of drawing of the fiber as a result of surface contamination, damage from handling, or the application of the protective coating.

It is necessary to estimate the maximum stress levels that can be tolerated by the fiber during handling and cabling. The standard practice is to screen-proof test fibers during the manufacturing process, up to a typical level of 300-500 gram-force. This testing helps to weed out any weak fibers that may have been produced. Fibers must also withstand a degree of static fatigue. Tests are performed by applying a present stress on sample fibers and measuring the time before failure.

Typical fibers are flexible enough to be wound around a finger. However, if permanent coils of fibers are installed in a system, sharp bends must be avoided so as to minimize the stress that may cause premature failure under long-term static fatigue conditions.[3]

Fabrication

The perform is fabricated by means of modified chemical vapour deposition (MCVD) process. Initially the substrate tube is cleaned by hydrofluoric acid and fire-polished to remove stress in the glass and later on etched with freon to remove surface impurities. The reactants ($SiCl_4$ + 0_2) are introduced at one end of the rotating tube while an exhaust is located at the other end. Cladding layer is made by deposition of materials such as $SiCl_4$, G_eCl_4 and $POCL_3$ in different environments such as oxygen, helium and Freon. During clad process, Freon reduced the refractive index of the clad and reaction converts halides into oxides. Approximately, 25-30 layers of cladding are deposited on the inside of the substrate tube. A core layer is deposited by means of compounds like $SiCl_4$, G_eCl_4 in gaseous environment of oxygen, helium and Freon. $GeCl_4$, converts to GeO_2, which serves as a dopant to increase the refractive index of the core layer, whereas helium lowers the deposition temperature[4]. The flow of reactants and the speed of traversing oxyhydrogen burner are closely monitored using a video camera. When the desired thickness is achieved, valve is closed to stop the flow of the reactants. After deposition of core layers on the inner side of tube this composite tube is heated to high temperature from outside so that it collapses to form a solid rod. The freon gas is passed while collapsing so that the core has higher refractive index than the clad as well as the solid glass rod becomes free of air bubbles. The chlorine gas is also used in combination with Freon so as to remove OH from SiO_2. This perform is subjected to fiber drawing process[5].

The reaction takes place during perform fabrication.

$SiCl_4 + SO_2 \rightarrow SiO_2 + 2Cl_2$: Conversion to quartz

$GeCl_4 + O_2 \rightarrow GeO_2 + 2Cl_2$: Alteration refraction

$4\,POCl_4 + 3O_2 \rightarrow 2P_2O_5 + 6Cl_2$: Alteration of refractive index

Freon (CCl_4F_2 on hearing forms the compound SiF_4 instead of SiO_2, which lowers the deposition rate of SiO_2. The typical diameter lies in the range of 25-60 mm and 600 = 800 mm in length.

Optical Cable

After the fiber has been drawn and coated, it is encased in a cable so as to be protected from prolonged stresses that can reduce its life.

Cable design involves more than finding a tough cover for the fibers. It must minimize the attenuation due to microbending that can be caused by the fiber pressing on any rough surface within the cable. Since the fiber and cable usually have different thermal expansion rates, low temperatures will cause buckling in fibers that are tightly confined; high temperatures may raise the fiber tension to an unacceptable level. Either condition would produce microbending and hence increased attenuation. A proper cable design should take these temperature-dependant problems into account and minimize, if not eliminate, their effects.

In addition, the cable should be light-weight, flexible and allow ready access to, and identification of, the fibers for splicing. The longer the length of the manufactured cable, the fewer would be the splices required in the field. Most important, the cable must be economical to be manufactured, installed and maintained[6].

Rayleigh Scattering Losses

Rayleigh scattering in glass is the same phenomenon that scatters light from the sun in the atmosphere and explains the formation of a blue sky. Rayleigh type of scattering of light takes placed due to the variations in the refractive index in glass.

The glass used in optical fiber is not a crystalline solid but an amorphous one. It is prepared by allowing glass to cool from the molten state at high temperatures until it freezes. When it is still plastic, glass is drawn out in tension into its fiber form. During the forming process following two defects may arise :

1. Glass being amorphous is composed of a randomly connected network of molecules. Such a structure naturally contains regions in which the molecular density is either higher or lower than the average density in the glass.

2. Since the glass is made up of several oxides, such as SiO_2, GeO_2 and P_2O_5, compositional fluctuation may occur.

The two effect give rise to the variations in refractive index which occurs within the glass over distances that are small compared to the wavelength of light. Submicroscopic variations in the glass density and doping impurities are frozen into glass during manufacture and they act as the reflecting and refracting facets to scatter a small portion of light passing through the glass. The careful manufacturing techniques are capable of reducing these anomalies to a minimum but they cannot be totally eliminated.

Structural inhomgeneities and defects are created during the fabrication of fiber and they can also cause the scattering of light out of the fiber. These defects may be in the form of trapped gas bubbles, unreacted starting materials, and crystallized regions in the glass.

In general, the perform manufacturing methods have been so improved that they have minimized these extrinsic effect to the point where the scattering arising form them is negligible compared to the intrinsic Rayleigh scattering.

The losses induced due to the scattering effect very inversely as the fourth power of wavelength (loss λ^{-4}) and the losses decrease dramatically with the increase of wavelength. For wavelengths below about 1μm it is the dominant loss mechanism in a fiber. These effect are reduced to loss than about 0.3 dB/km at a wavelength of 1.3μm. Fig .2.1 shows the variation of the intrinsic scattering losses in silica fiber glass with wavelength over the usable portion of the spectrum from 0.7 to 1.6 μm wavelength.

For a single component glass (1) the Rayleigh scattering coefficient τ_R is given by[7]

$$\tau_R = \frac{8\pi^3}{3\lambda^4} n_1^8 p^2 B_c K_B T_F \qquad ...(2.3)$$

Where τ_R is the Rayleigh coffeicient, λ is the wave length of the optical radiation, n_1 is the refractive index of the medium, p is the average photoelastic coefficient, B_c is the isothermal compressibility at a fictive temperature T_F and K_B is the Boltzmann constant.

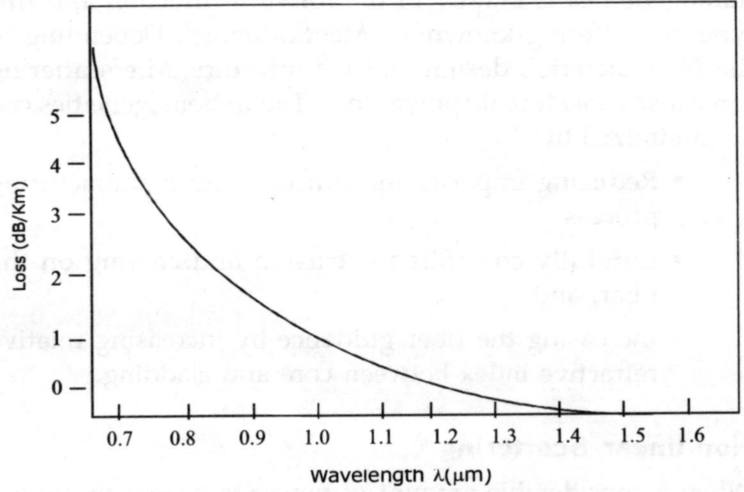

Fig. 2.1 : A typical curve for the variation of Rayleigh scattering losses in dB/km as function of wavelength in μm.

The fricative temperature of glass is define as the temperature at which glass can reach a state of thermal equilibrium and closely related to the anneal temperature. Again the Rayleigh scatting coefficient τ_R is related to the transmission loss factor (transmission) of the fiber denoted by the following relationship :

$$= \exp(-\tau_R L) \qquad \text{...(2.4)}$$

Where L is the length of the fiber. It is apparent from Eq.(2.4) that the fundamental components of Rayleigh scattering reduced considerably by operating at the longest wavelength.

MIE Scattering

Linear scattering may occur at in homogeneities which are comparable to in size with the guided wavelength. When the size of scattering in homogeneities is greater than $\lambda/10$, the scattered intensity has an angular dependence and can be quite large. The scattering occurring due to such in homogeneities is mainly in the forward direction and this type of scattering known as *'Mie Scattering'*. Depending in the fiber material, design and manufacture, Mie scattering can cause considerable power loss. The in homogeneities can be minimized by

- Reducing imperfection during glass manufacturing process
- Carefully controlled extrusion and coating on the fiber, and
- Increasing the fiber guidance by increasing relative refractive index between core and cladding.

Non-linear Scattering

When a considerable amount of power is passed through a fiber, a high value of electric field leads to the presence of non-liner scattering. Such scattering causes a significant power loss to be scattered in forward, backward or side way directions depending on the nature of interaction. A frequency shift of scattered light is associated with the non-linear scattering. The important non-linear scattering are: Brillouin Scattering and Raman Scattering.

The power density is defined as the power per unit area and at normal power density the non-linear interactions are negligible but as a higher power density a significant amount of energy may be removed by light wave. Such power may be encountered with more powerful laser diode through a small fiber core.

Stimulated Brillouin Scattering

Brilllouin scattering may be regarded as the modulation of light through thermal molecular vibration with the fiber. The incident photos of light undergoes non-linear to produce vibrational energy or 'phonons' in the glass as well as the scattering light is found to be frequency modulated by the thermal energy, and both upward and downward frequency shifts are observed. The amount of the frequency shift and the strength of scattering vary as the function of the scattering angle maximum occurring in the backward direction and the minimum or zero being observed in the forward direction. Thus Brillouin scattering occurs mainly in the backward direction which direction the power to the sources (i.e. from receiver) and the power in the receiver is reduced.

The optical power level at which brillouin scattering becomes significant in a single mode fiber is given by empirical formulae. The threshold power level P_B is given by[8]

$$P_B = 4.4 \times 10^{-3} d^2 \lambda^2 \alpha_{db} \Delta\tau \text{ Watts} \quad ...(2.5)$$

Where d and λ are the core diameter and operating wavelength of the fiber respectively and both measured in micrometer, α_{dB} is the fiber attenuation in dB/km. $\Delta\tau$ is the source bandwidth (*i.e.* injection laser) in giga-Hertz. The above equation enables us to determine the threshold power which must be launched in a single mode fiber before stimulated Brillouin scattering occurs.

Stimulated Raman Scattering

The non-linear interaction in Raman scattering produces a high frequency phonon and a scattered photon, whereas low frequency phonons are produced in Brillouin scattering. In Raman scattering the scattered light is predominantly in the forward direction and thus the power is not reduced in the receiver.

The threshold power level for the significant Raman scattering to occur is given by

$$P_B = 5.9 \times 10^{-2} d^2 \lambda \alpha_{dB} \Delta\tau \text{ Watts} \quad ...(2.6)$$

Where d is the diameter of the fiber core in μm is the wavelength emitted by the source in μm is the fiber loss in dB/km and P_R is the threshold optical power.

Non-linear Scattering and Frequency Shift

The frequency shift associated with the inelastic scattering can be quite small (less than 1 cm^{-1}) in Brillouin scattering where the frequency shifts occur due to acoustic phonon. In the case of Raman scattering large frequency shifts greater than 100 cm^{-1} are observed and in this case shifts occur due to the molecular vibration optical frequency phonon. The important feature of inelastic scattering processes is that they not only result in a frequency shift but for a sufficiently high intensity of the incident optical power they exhibit an optical gain at the shifted frequency. The incident optical frequency is known as the pump frequency (W_p) that gives two shifted frequency components known as strokes (W_s) and antistoke's (W_a) components or the radiation.

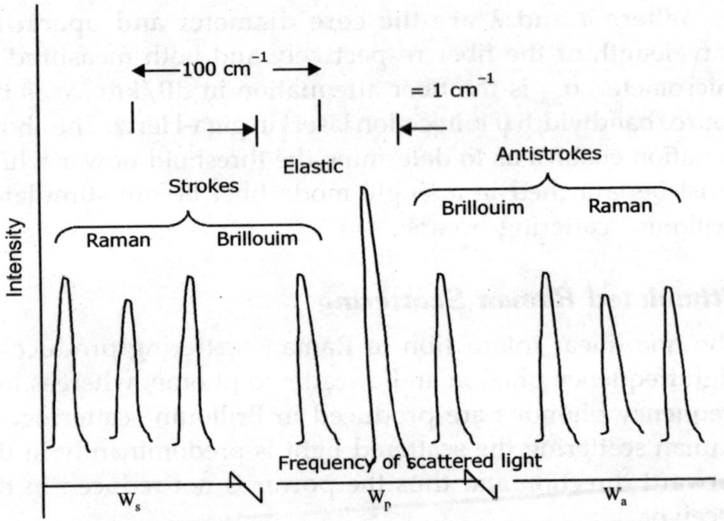

Fig. 2.2 : Spectrum of scattered light showing in elastic scattering process.

For a typical fiber the power of the pump frequency around a watt in hundred metres of fiber results in a Raman gain of about a factor of 2. By contrast the peak Brillouin gain is much greater than the Raman gain but the Brillouin frequency shift and gain-bandwidth are much smaller. Moreover, Brillouin gain only exist for the propagation of light in opposite direction to that of pump light while Raman amplification will occur for light propagation in either direction. Fig. 2.2 shows the spectrum of scattered light illustrating inelastic processes. The intensity of the anti stoke Raman lines is far less than that of stokes Raman lines.

Absorption Losses

There are three mechanisms that contribute to the absorption losses. There are : (1) Ultraviolet absorption; (2) Infrared absorption; and (3) Ion resonance absorption.

Ultra Violet Absorption

Ultraviolet absorption takes place, because for fused silica valance electrons absorb light and can be ionized to conduction electrons with a center wavelength of about 0.14μm. This wavelength corresponds to the energy level of about 8.5 eV. This ionization gives rise to an energy loss in the light fields and contributes to the transmission loss in the fiber. This absorption does not only occur at this fixed wavelength but takes place over a broad band of frequencies up to the visible portion of the spectrum. This absorption loss decreases with the increase of the wavelength. The UV absorption 'tail' falls off causing a negligible amount of loss in the wavelength band from 1.2 to 1.3 μm. The ultra-violet edge of the electron absorption band in both crystalline and amorphous materials follows the following empirical relationship.

$$\alpha_{uv} = Ce^{E/E_0} \qquad ...(2.7)$$

Which is known ad Urbach's rules. Here C and E_0 are empirical constants. E is the photon energy. α_{uv} = attenuation constant in the ultra violet region.

In order to modify the refractive index of fiber, glass is purposely doped with induced impurities. Such as germanium dioxide. The refractive index of glass increases with the amount of dopant. The presence of the impurity causes some increase in the UV absorption tail, because of an upward shift in the wavelength of the UV absorption peak. The typical value of loss at 1.2 μm wavelength for most fibers does not exceed 0.1 dB/km. Fig. 2.3 shows the absorption tail for pure silica glass and germanium doped silica glass.

Infra-red Absorption

Infra-red absorption occurs because the photons of light energy are absorbed by atoms within the glass molecules and converted to random mechanical random vibrations typical of heating. For silica glass the IR absorption exhibits a main spectral peak at 8 μm with the minor peaks at 3.3, 3.8 and 4.4 μm. Again the peaks are broad falling off in the visible portion of the spectrum and the typical values of losses at the wavelength of 1.5 μm are less than 0.5 dB/km. Fig. 2.3 shows typical infra-red absorption for silica glass in the usable range.

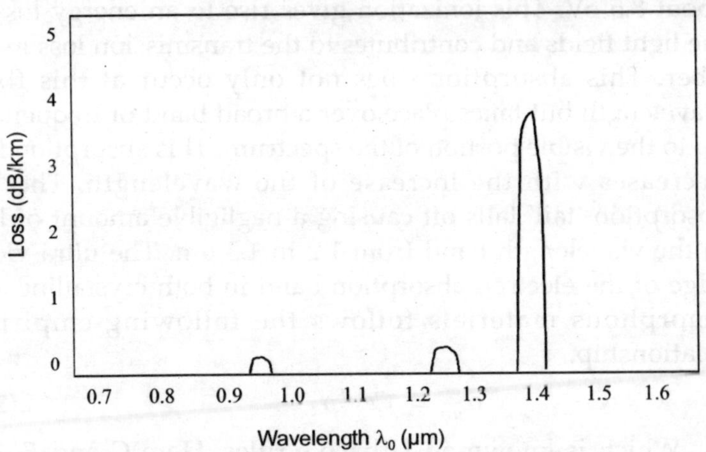

Fig. 2.3 : Absorption loss effect in pure glass silica fibers: Graphs for the variation of loss in dB/km with wavelength in μm.

Ion-Resonance Absorption

Minutes quantities of water molecules may be trapped in the glass at the time of manufacture and these contribute OH-ions to the materials. The OH-ions exhibit absorption peaks at 0.95, 1.25 and 1.39 μm. When it is desired that these peaks are not to spread and merge to predominate the loss spectrum of the fiber the water content of the glass has to be kept below 0.01 parts per million parts. Fig. 2.3 shows the three peaks with a typical value for a low-loss fiber.

The presence of some other metals and impurities may give rise to undesirable losses within the usable portion of the spectrum. The presence of some impurities like iron, copper and chromium is to be avoided. In order to reduce the presence of these impurities to acceptable levels good refining technique for purifying raw materials must be followed. Zone refining technique which is usually used for preparing pure silicon chips for integrated circuits is usually employed.

Bending Losses

Radiative losses occur whenever an optical fiber undergoes a bend of finite radius of curvature. Fibers an be subjected to two types of bends :

1. Microbendings are the random microscopic bends of the fiber axis that can arise when the fibers are incorporated into cables.
2. Constant Radius Bending or Microbendings these are the bends having radii that are large compared to the fiber diameter, for example, such bends when a fiber cable turns a corner.

Microbending

Microbending is a microscopic bending with repetative changes in the axis of the core of the fiber (*Fig. 2.4*) and it takes place due to the slightly different contraction rate between the core and the cladding materials. Micorbending occurs due to non uniform lateral pressure created during the cabling of the fiber.

When the fibers are subsequently would on a multiplayer cable or wound on spool for transportation of the fiber from

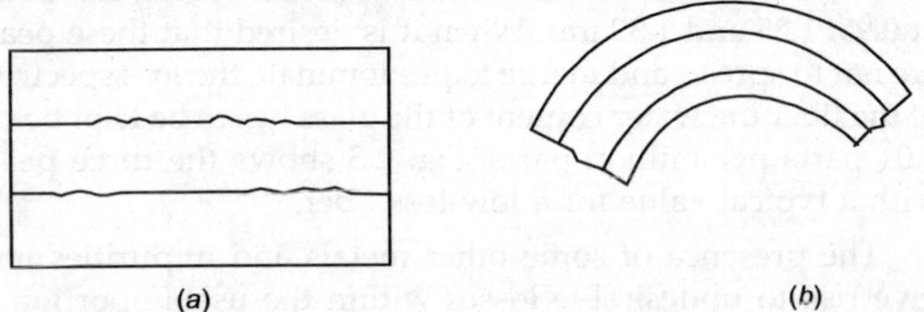

Fig. 2.4 : Examples of (a) microbend and (b) macrobends are highly exaggerated in size in this figure.

one place to other, then microbending can also be introduced into the fiber. Losses due to microbending takes place, because the small bends acts as the scattering facets and these facets causes mode coupling to occur. Energy from the guided modes is cross coupled to the leaky mode and is lost through the cladding. Microbendings are randomly distributed over the length of the fiber and the losses due to them will be uniformly distributed so that the total amount of loss for a fiber can be determined. Careful precautions in manufacturing and handling of fibers will be able to reduce these losses. One method of minimizing the microbending losses is done by extruding a compressible jacket over the fiber. When external forces are applied to this configuration, the jacket will be deformed, but the fiber will tend to stay relatively straight as shown in Fig. 2.5.

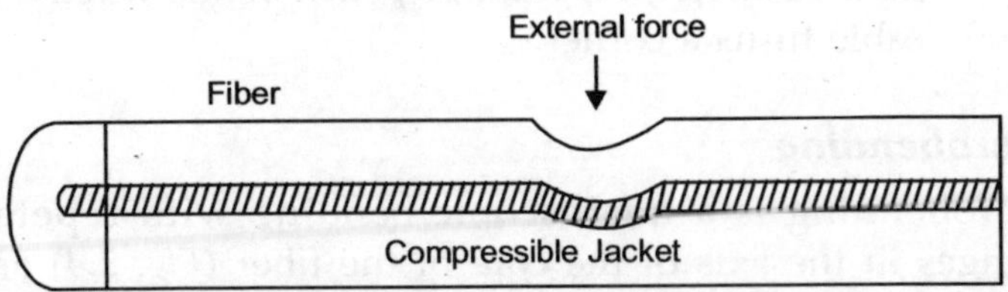

Fig. 2.5 : A Compressible Jacket extruded over the fiber minimizes microbending resulting from external forces

Constant Radius Bending

When the optical fibers are installed in cable ducts or on a pole for a transmission line, it is necessary to introduce bends in the fiber to join corners. Sometime these bends may be quite sharp. For example, at a pole hanger point where the cable has sag between two poles or at right angle turns in building conduits, the sag is quite sharp. These large radius bends will also introduce some loss of light energy in the fiber.

Fig. 2.6 illustrates the manner in which a bend introduces a loss in a fiber. In the figure a ray of light which is fully guided, reaches the reflection point *A* at an angle θ_A. If the fiber were not bent, it arrives at B_1 as the next reflection point. But with the bend in the fiber, the ray encounters the fiber wall early at the outside edge of the bend at point B_2 at an incidence angle θ_B. The angle θ_B is smaller than angle θ_A in the straight section. When angle θ_B is smaller than the critical angle, the ray will manage to escape from the fiber core and some of the energy in the corresponding mode will be lost. If a bare fiber is bent sharply, the light escaping from the core can be observed as a bright light in the form of a line long the outer edge of the fiber bend.

A sharp bend is responsible for more modes to occur and light to escape at the bend. When a fiber is installed, it is necessary to ensure that no sharp bends are going to occur.

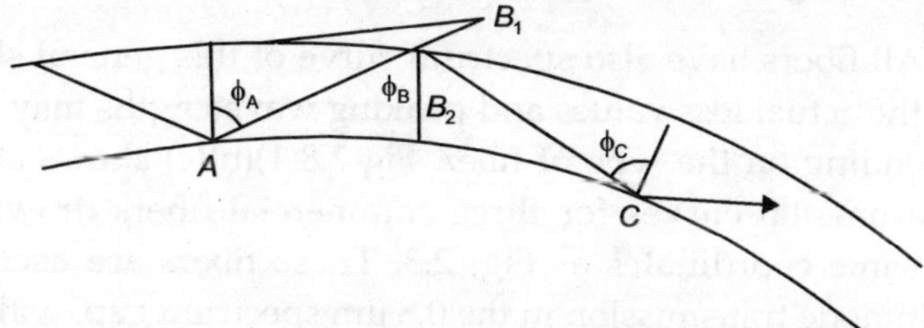

Fig. 2.6 : Loss due to ray propagation in a bent fiber

Combined Losses in Fibers

Now we can summarize the three types of inherent to a fiber. These are: (2) Rayleigh scattering losses; (2) material absorption losses; (3) losses due to mode coupling because of scattering.

During manufacturing process this must be reduced to a minimum. Of course, losses due to Rayleigh scattering and material absorption are predominant and every step should be taken during manufacture to reduce these losses. Fig 2.7 shows that losses in a typical multimode fiber as a function of wavelength so that the losses due to Rayleigh scattering and material absorption can be compared. This fiber has relatively low losses compared to some other fiber which may have a loss as high as 20 dB/km.

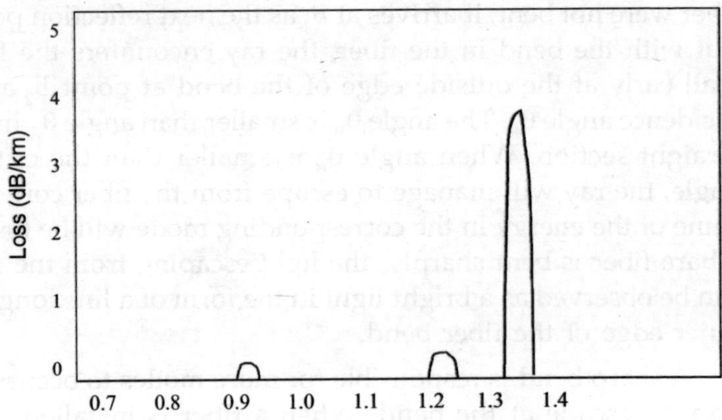

Fig. 2.7 : Total spectrum of a typical optical fiber

All fibers have also spectrum curve of this general shape but the actual loss values and peaking wavelengths may vary depending on the type of fiber. Fig 2.8(1)(b)(c) shows actual experimental curves for three commercial fibers drawn on the same coordinates as Fig. 2.3. These fibers are used for multimode transmission in the 0.8 μm spectrum gap, with the information specified for the range 0-.5 to 1.1 μm instead of 0.7 to 1.6 μm wavelength band. All of the curves have a 'window' in the spectrum of losses at about 0.8μm which coincides with the spectral output of many LED sources especially available for fiber communications. Within the window, losses at their lowest, typically between 5 to 10 dB/km. Other spectrum windows occur at 1.2 μm and at 1.3 μm in the typical spectra for step index glass-clad fibers and since this lies within the gap between the ultraviolet and infrared tails, the lowest possible losses for any fibers can be obtained window. Typical losses are in the order of 0.5 to 2 dB/km that can be obtained in carefully designed fibers. These fibers are used for long distance monomode transmission system with widely spaced repeaters.

Critical Radius of a Bend

The optical fiber suffers losses due to radiation at the bends. Fig. 2.8d shows an illustration of this situation. The part of the mode which is situated outside the bend is required to propagate faster than that on the inside so that the wave front perpendicular to the direction of propagation is maintained. Thus, the part of the mode in the cladding is required to travel faster than the velocity of light in that medium. Since this is not possible the energy associated with this part of the mode is lost through radiation. This loss can be represented by a radiation attenuation coefficient α_r. The relationship between the radius of curvature of the bend and α_r is given by[9].

$$\alpha_r = C_1 \exp(-C_2 R) \quad \text{...(2.8)}$$

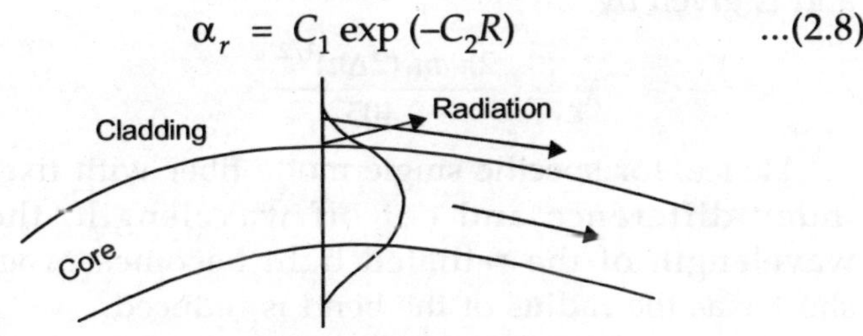

Fig. 2.8 : Curvature of the fiber

Where R is the radius of curvature of the fiber bend, and C_1 and C_2 are the constants which are independent of R. Moreover, large bending losses tend to occur in multi mode fiber at a critical radius of curvature R_c which may be calculated from the following relationship[9]

$$R_c = \frac{3n_1^2\lambda}{4\pi(n_1^2 - n_2^2)^{3/2}} \quad ...(2.9)$$

When n_1 and n_2 are the refractive indices of the core and cladding of the fiber respectively.

In may be noted from the above expression that the potential microbending may be minimized by :

(*a*) Designing fibers with large relative refractive index difference between the core and cladding.

(*b*) Operating at the shortest possible wavelength.

The above criteria for minimizing the bending losses can be applied to single mode fiber. One theory based on single quasi-guided mode gives an expression from which the critical radius of curvature for a single mode fiber R_{cs} can be determined. The expression for the critical radius of curvature is given by[10]

$$R_{cs} = \frac{20\lambda}{(n_1 - n_2)^{3/2}}\left(2.748 - 0.996\frac{\lambda}{\lambda_c}\right)^{-3} \quad ...(2.10)$$

Where λ_c is the cut off wavelength of the single modefiber and is given by

$$\lambda_c = \frac{2\pi\, an_1(2\Delta n)^{1/2}}{2.405} \quad ...(2.11)$$

Hence, for specific single mode fiber with fixed relative index difference and cut off wavelength, the critical wavelength of the radiated light becomes progressively shorter as the radius of the bend is reduced.

REFERENCES

1. Bela, A.L., 'Introduction to Laser Physics', John Wiley and Sons, Inc. N.Y. 1966.
2. S.Ramabhadran 'Telecommunications Principles Circuits Systems and Experiments' Khanna Publishers, Delhi, (887-888), 2002.

3. S.Ramabhadran 'Telecommunications Principles Circuits Systems and Experiments' Khanna Publishers, Delhi, (888), 2002.
4. Fleming JW, 'Fiber Optics Technicians Hand Book' by Jim Hayer, Delmar Publisher's Albany, New York, Electron Lett. 14 (326), 1978.
5. Vivek P Kude and R.S.Khairnar Bull Mat Sci., Vol. 27, 2004
6. S. Ramabhadran 'Telecommunications Principles Circuits Systems and Experiments' Khanna Publishers, Delhi (890), 2002.
7. Rolshansky, 'Propagation in Glass Optical Wave Guides,' Rev. Mod. Phys., 51(2), (341-3367)
8. MM Ramsay and G.A. Hochham, Propagation in Optical Fiber Waveguide.
9. H.F. Wolf, Optical Waveguide in H.F. Wolf Edition Handbook Fiber Optics, Theory and Applications,(43-152),1979.
10. W.A.Gambling, H.Matsumura and G.M.Ragdale, Curvature and Microbending Losses in Single Mode Optical, Opt Quantum Electronics, (43-59), 1979.

3

EFFECT OF DISPERSION ON PULSE TRANSMISSION

Introduction

It may be noted that a light pulse with a given width and amplitude injected into one end of a fiber should arrive at its other end with the shape and width unchanged, and only its amplitude is reduced by losses. If the losses are extremely large, the pulse amplitude at the receiving end will be small to be detected and a repeater has to be included to boost up the signal before its entering into next section.

Several dispersion effects are encountered by the pulse of light propagating through a fiber and these act to spread out the pulse in the time domain changing the shape of the pulse. As a result, the pulse may be got merged in the previous or in the succeeding pulses becoming indistinguishable at the receiver as illustrated in Fig. 3.1. The effect is known as inter symbol interference (ISI). The pulses may be separated by increasing the time interval between pulses, but thereby the maximum bit rate will be reduced.[1]

There are three kinds of dispersion due to three separate mechanisms existing in the fiber. These are: (1) Intermodal

Dispersion or Multipath dispersion; (2) Material or chromatic dispersion; and (3) waveguide dispersion.

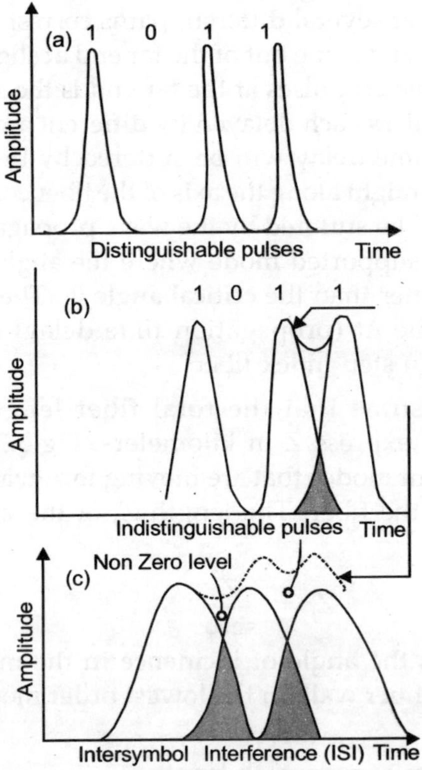

Fig. 3.1 : An illustration of puls broadcning. The broadening of the light pulses occurs as they are transmitted through the fiber producing intersymbol interference (ISI) (*a*) fiber input, (*b*) the output pulse of the fiber at distance L_1 (*c*) fiber output at a distance L_2 where $L_2 > L_1$.

Intermodal or Multipath Dispersion

The effective group velocity of light wave is different for each mode that wave guide will support, even though the phase velocity in different mode ray may be indentical. This happens because total path followed by a ray, in each of the mode is zigzag in nature and the path in a particular mode has different total length than each of the other mode rays.

When a pulse of light is transmitted in a fiber, it will be propagated over several different paths corresponding to the excited modes and come out of the far end at slightly different times. The received pulses at the far end is the summation of these mode pulses each delayed by different amount of time. The shortest time delay will be suffered by the plane wave propagating straight along the axis of the fiber core: the longest time delay will be suffered by the wave propagating with the highest order supported mode where the angle of incidence is slightly greater than the critical angle θ_c. The difference in the arrival time Δt (propagation time delay) can easily be calculated for a step index fiber[2].

Let us assume that the total fiber length is Z. It is convenient to express Z in kilometers. Fig 3.2. Shows two rays of different modes that are moving in zigzag paths along the length of the fiber. The length Z_t of the zigzag path is found to be

$$Z_t = \frac{Z}{\sin\phi} \qquad ...(3.1)$$

When ϕ is the angle of incidence in the mode with the normal to the fiber wall. In the lowest order mode, $\phi = \phi_{max} = 90°$.

Thus, the minimum path length

$$Z_t = \frac{Z}{\sin\phi_{max}} = \frac{Z}{\sin 90°} = Z \qquad ...(3.2)$$

and ϕ_{min} the longest path is found to be maximum path length,

$$Z_{tmax} = \frac{Z}{\sin\phi_{min}} = \frac{Z}{\sin\theta_c} = Z\frac{n_1}{n_2} \qquad ...(3.3)$$

The maximum path difference ΔZ in the path due to modal separation is found to be

$$\Delta Z = Z_{tmax} - Z_{tmax} = Z\left(\frac{n_1}{n_2} - 1\right) = Z\left(\frac{n_1 - n_2}{n_2}\right) \qquad ...(3.4)$$

The maximum path difference depends on the difference of refractive index between the core and the cladding. Since the light ray in the fiber is propagating through a dielectric medium with a dielectric constant which is greater than unity, the ray travels more slowly than that they would move in free space. It is assumed that the relative permeability of the dielectric medium is unity. The phase velocity in the dielectric along the ray path is

Phase velocity

$$V_p = \frac{1}{\sqrt{\mu\varepsilon}} = \frac{1}{\sqrt{\mu_0\varepsilon_0}} = \frac{1}{\sqrt{\mu_r\varepsilon_r}} = \frac{C}{\sqrt{\varepsilon_r}} (\mu_r = 1) \qquad ...(3.5)$$

Since $C = \frac{1}{\sqrt{\mu_0\varepsilon_0}}$ velocity of light in free space = 3×10^8 m/s thus the dielectric constant ε_r is

$$\sqrt{\varepsilon_r} = \frac{C}{V_P} = n = \text{refractive index of the medium} \qquad ...(3.6)$$

Thus, we find that the relationship between the dielectric refractive index n_1 is given by

$$\varepsilon_r = n^2 \qquad ...(3.7)$$

The phase velocity in the glass core of the fiber with refractive index n_1 is given by

$$\text{Phase velocity}, V_{P(\text{glass})} = \frac{C}{n_1} \qquad ...(3.8)$$

Finally, the maximum difference in the time delay between the rays of highest and lowest order modes is obtained by dividing the difference in the path length by the phase velocity. Denoting this by t and is given by

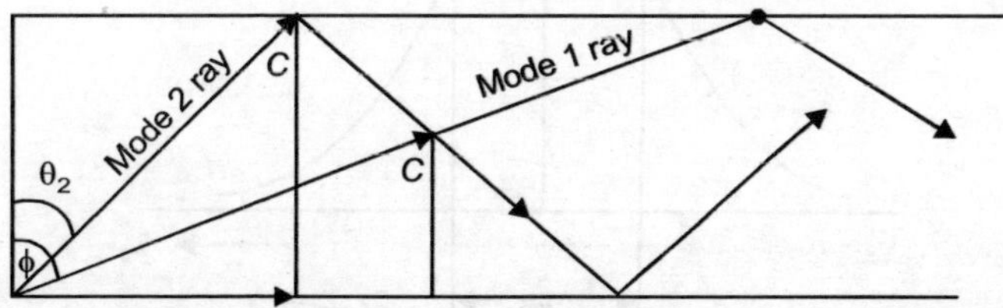

Fig. 3.2 : Two rays of different modes removing in a zigzag paths along a fiber

$$\Delta t = \frac{\Delta z}{V_P} = \frac{n_1 Z}{C}\left(\frac{n_1 - n_2}{n_2}\right) = \left(\frac{Z}{C}\right)\left(\frac{n_1(n_1 - n_2)}{n_2}\right) \quad ...(3.9)$$

Denoting the difference between the refractive indices at the core and cladding $(n_1 - n_2)$ by Δn, the maximum time difference between becomes

$$\Delta t = \frac{Z}{C}\frac{n_1}{n_2}\Delta n \quad ...(3.10)$$

or

$$\frac{\Delta t}{Z} = \frac{n_1}{n_2 C}\Delta n \quad ...(3.10)$$

The term $\Delta t/Z$ is known as the 'multiple time difference' of the fiber.

Material Dispersion

The refractive index of core glass of fiber is not the same for lights of different wavelengths but it depends on the wavelength of light in a complicated way. When a pulse of light transmitted contains components of several wavelengths centered about a center wavelength as shown in fig 3.3. The pulse component having shorter wavelengths will experience move delay that those of larger wavelengths. As a result there is an effective time dispersion of the pulse at the receiving end of the fiber[3,5].

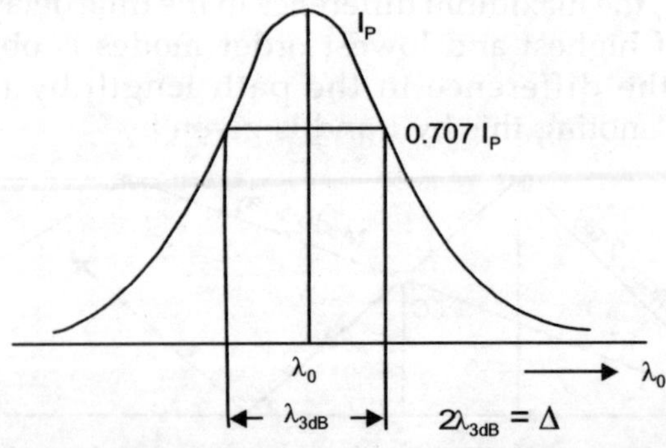

Fig. 3.3 : Defining the spectral width of the light sources : Central wavelength λ_0 : $2\lambda_{3dB} = \Delta$

Relationship Between the Material Dispersion and Wavelengths

Material dispersion is due to the explicit dependence of the refractive index of the core cladding on the wavelength (λ_o). It is a characteristic of the material only. Material dispersion plays a very important role in design of a fiber optics communication system. When a temporal pulse passes through a homogeneous medium, it propagates with a group velocity (V_g) given by

$$1/V_g = dk/dw \quad ...(3.11)$$

$$\Rightarrow \quad \frac{1}{V_g} = \frac{d}{dw}(K) \quad ...(3.12)$$

$$= \frac{d}{dw}\left(\frac{n}{c}n(w)\right) \quad ...(3.13)$$

Where $k(w) \equiv \frac{n}{c}n(w)$, $n(w) \equiv$ frequency–dependent refractive index.

In terms of wavelength, the group velocity becomes

$$\frac{1}{V_g} = \frac{1}{c}\left(n(\lambda_0) - (\lambda_0)\frac{dn}{d\lambda_0}\right) \quad ...(3.14)$$

Thus, the time taken by a pulse to traverse length L of fiber is given by

$$\tau = \tau(\lambda_0) = \frac{L}{V_g} = \frac{L}{c}\left(n(\lambda_0) - (\lambda_0)\frac{dn}{d\lambda_0}\right) \quad ...(3.15)$$

Hence, temporal broadening of the pulse is

$$\nabla\tau = \frac{d_\tau}{d\lambda_0}\nabla\lambda_0 = -\left(\frac{L}{C}\lambda_0^2\right)\frac{d^2n}{d\lambda_0^2}\left(\frac{\nabla\lambda_0}{\lambda_0}\right) \quad ...(3.16)$$

The above broadening is referred to as material dispersion. Material dispersion in terms of ps/km-nm.

$$D_m = \frac{1}{\lambda_0 C}\left(\lambda_0^2\frac{d^2n}{d\lambda_0^2}\right)\left(\frac{\nabla\lambda_0}{\lambda_0}\right)10^9 \text{ ps/km-nm} \quad ...(3.17)$$

Where λ_0 is measured in micro meters.

Combined Effect of Material Dispersion and Intermodal Dispersion

In estimating the bandwidth and maximum bit rate of an optical communication channel we need to consider the shape and width of the receive pulse. The shape on the arrival of an impulse that has been broadened by material dispersion will control the power distribution among the wavelengths making up the pulse. We shall find in general that most optical sources have distribution of power with wavelengths that are roughly Gaussian in nature. We should then expect the receive pulse shape to take on a similar Gaussian form about the mean arrival time t as shown if fig. 3.4 (*a*), (*b*) Now let us

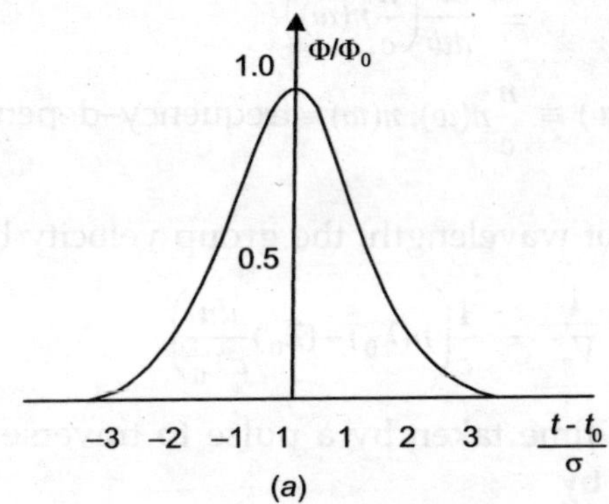

Fig. 3.4. (*a*). Power Distribution

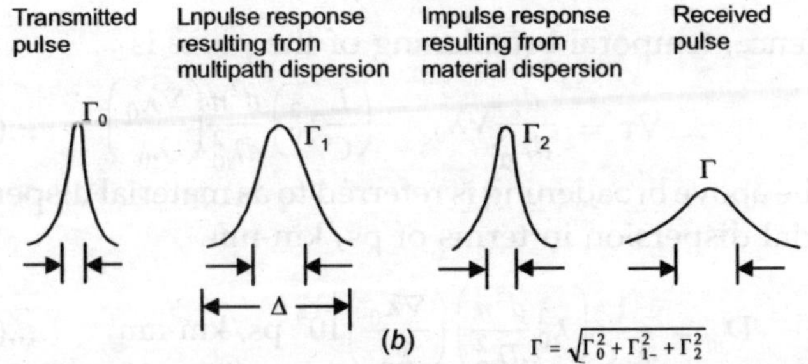

Fig. 3.4 (*b*). Gaussian wave

assume that the impulse is broadened by both material and multi path dispersions, and that the two mechanisms are uncorrelated and they independently lead to approximately Gaussian pulses having their half height pulse width Γ_1 and Γ_2 respectively. The two mechanisms will then combine to produce pulse which remains roughly Gaussian in shape and which will have a half width which is given by

$$\Gamma = \sqrt{\Gamma_1^2 + \Gamma_2^2} \qquad \text{....(3.18)}$$

When the transmitted pulse is not an impulse to start with but is also a Gaussian with a full width at the half height value of Γ_0, then we may extend this argument as illustrated in Fig 3.5 to suggest that Γ becomes

$$v = \frac{w}{c} a\sqrt{n_1^2 - n_2^2}\ \Gamma = \sqrt{\Gamma_0^2 + \Gamma_1^2 + \Gamma_2^2} \qquad \text{...(3.19)}$$

Where Γ_0 is the width, Γ_1 is the half height pulse width that would result from multi path broadening alone and Γ_2 represents the broadening due to material dispersion alone.

Wave Guide Dispersion

When a fiber could be so operated that the multipath and material dispersions are all eliminated as should be the case for a single mode fiber operation near $\lambda = 1.3\ \mu m$, then a third dispersion mechanism will predominate except in the case ideally monochromatic light. Unfortunately ideal monochromatic courses are not available so that the light transmitted consists of component of several wavelengths near the central wavelength λ_0 within an envelope like that in Fig 3.5 . The result is that the constant phase wave front separation as illustrated in Fig. 3.5 will be slightly different for different wavelengths and the corresponding angle of incidence will also be slightly different. This will cause a corresponding shift in the group velocity. The group velocity varies in complicated way with the wavelength and the net result is the broadening of the received pulse. This effect is only the result of the guiding characteristics of the fiber and hence it is known as the 'wave guide dispersion'.

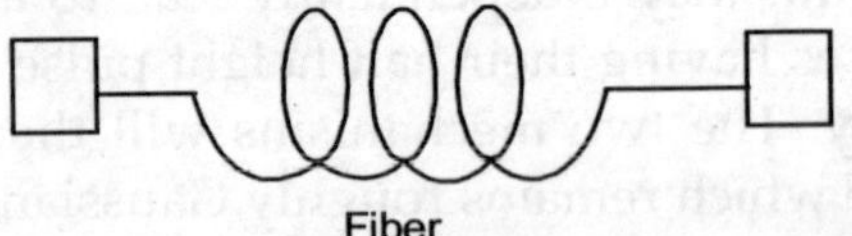

Fig. 3.5 : Dispersive effect in combination

Waveguide Dispersion—Equations

Wave guide dispersion is due to the explicit dependence of the refractive index of the core and cladding on the frequency (w). In case of wave guide dispersion, wave propagation vector

$$\beta = \frac{w}{c}[n_2 + (n_1 - n_2)b(v)] \quad ....(3.20)$$

Where b-normalized propagation constant, $v = \frac{w}{c} a\sqrt{n_1^2 - n_2^2}$

The waveguide parameter, a is the radius of the core, n_1 and n_2 are the core and cladding refractive index.

Hence, group velocity is given by

$$\frac{1}{V_g} = \frac{d\beta}{dW} = \frac{n_2}{c} + \frac{n_1 - n_2}{c}\left(\frac{d}{dv}(bv)\right) \quad ...(3.21)$$

Thus, the time taken by a pulse to traverse length L of the fiber is given by

$$\tau_w \frac{L}{Vg} = \frac{L}{C} n_2 \left(1 + \Delta \frac{d}{dv}(bv)\right) \quad ...(3.22)$$

Where

$$\Delta = \frac{n_1^2 - n_2^2}{2n^2 1} \cong \frac{n_1 - n_2}{n_2} \quad ...(3.23)$$

For a source having a spectral width $\Delta\lambda_0$, the corresponding waveguide dispersion is given by

$$\Delta\tau_w \frac{d\tau}{d\lambda} \Delta\lambda_0 \approx \frac{L}{C} n_2 \Delta \left(\frac{\Delta\lambda_0}{\lambda_0}\right) v \left(\frac{d^2(bv)}{dv^2}\right) \quad ...(3.24)$$

In terms of ps/km-nm, the waveguide dispersion is given by

$$D_w \frac{n_2\Delta}{c\lambda_0}\left(v\frac{d^2(bv)}{dv^2}\right)10^7 \text{ ps/km.nm} \qquad \text{...(3.25)}$$

Where λ_0

$$v\left(\frac{d^2(bv)}{dv^2}\right) = \frac{2B^2}{dv^2} \qquad \text{...(3.26)}$$

For a step index fiber the dispersion coefficient resulting from wave guide dispersion mechanism has a peak value of about 0.6 ps/nm. The value is an ideal lower limit on the dispersion at the wavelength where the material dispersion disappears. A partial cancellation does take place between the material dispersion and wave guide dispersion which has a zero corss point as shown in Fig. 3.5 slightly higher wavelength. By turning the light source and keeping the bandwith now it is possible to remain practical value of loss less than 6.6. ps/km.

Effect of Non-linearity in Dispersion Compensation Fiber

Here it has been treated that the optical fiber as a non-linear medium, that is intensity dependent refractive index. Consider the propagation of an optical pulse in a lossy fiber characterized by the refractive index.

$$n(w) = n_o(w) + n_{20}I, \qquad \text{...(3.27)}$$

where $n_o(w)$ is the linear part of the refracting index, $n_{20}I$ is the intensity-dependent non-linear part.

In case of material dispersion, if it use non-linear effect, the group velocity (v_g) is given by

$$\frac{1}{v_g} = \frac{dk}{dw} = \frac{d}{dw}\left[\frac{w}{c}n(w)\right], \qquad \text{...(3.28)}$$

where $k = \frac{w}{c}n(w)$,

$$\frac{1}{v_g} = \frac{d}{dw}\left[\frac{w}{c}n_o(w)+n_{20}I\}\right], \qquad \text{... (3.29)}$$

$$\frac{1}{v_g} = \frac{1}{c}\left[n_o(w)+n_{20}I+w\left(\frac{dn_o}{dw}+I\frac{dn_{20}}{dw}\right)\right] \qquad \text{...(3.30)}$$

Now, group velocity in terms of the free space wavelength $\lambda_0(=2\pi c/w)$ is given by

$$\frac{1}{v_g} = \frac{1}{c}\left[n_o(\lambda_0)+n_{20}I+\lambda_o\frac{dn_0}{d\lambda_0}-\lambda_0\frac{dn_{20}}{d\lambda_0}\right]. \qquad \text{...(3.31)}$$

Hence, the time taken by the pulse to traverse length L of the fiber is given by

$$\tau = \tau(\lambda_0) = \frac{L}{v_g}\left[n_o(\lambda_0)+n_{20}I+\lambda_0\frac{dn_0}{d\lambda_0}-\lambda_0\frac{dn_{20}}{d\lambda_0}\right]. \qquad \text{...(3.32)}$$

If the spectral width of the source is $\Delta\lambda_0$, the temporal broadening of the pulse is given by

$$\nabla\tau = \frac{d\tau}{d\lambda_0}\nabla\lambda_0 = \frac{L}{c}\left[\lambda_0\frac{d^2n_0}{d\lambda_0^2}+\lambda_0 I\frac{d^2n_{20}}{d\lambda_0^2}\right] = \frac{L}{c}\left[\lambda_0^2\left\{\frac{d^2n_0}{d\lambda_0^2}+\frac{d^2n_{20}}{d\lambda_0^2}I\right\}\left(\frac{\nabla\lambda_0}{\lambda_0}\right)\right] \qquad \text{...(3.33)}$$

We know

$$n_{20} = \frac{3\chi^3}{4c\in_0 n_0^2}, \qquad \text{...(3.34)}$$

$$\frac{d^2n_{20}}{d\lambda_0^2} = +\frac{9\chi^3}{2c\in_0 n_0^4}\frac{d^2n_0}{d\lambda_0^2} = \frac{6n_{20}}{n_0^2} \qquad \text{...(3.35)}$$

$$\text{Thus,}\quad \Delta\tau_0 = \frac{L}{c}\left[\left(\lambda_0^2\frac{d^2n_0}{d\lambda_0^2}\right)\left\{1+\frac{6n_{20}}{n_0^2}I\right\}\right]\left(\frac{\nabla\lambda_0}{\lambda_0}\right), \qquad \text{...(3.36)}$$

$$D_{mn} = \frac{10^9}{\lambda_0 c}\left[\left(\lambda_0^2\frac{d^2n_0}{d\lambda_0^2}\right)\left\{1+\frac{6n_{20}}{n_0^2}I\right\}\right], ps/km-nm. \qquad \text{...(3.37)}$$

In case of waveguide dispersion, it is considered that v (waveguide parameter) is approximately constant. Then

$$D_{mn} = \frac{n_2}{n_2}(n_0 + n_{20}I - n_2)\frac{10^2}{3\lambda_0}\left(\frac{d^2(bv)}{dv^2}\right),$$

$$D_{mn} = \frac{n_2\nabla}{c\lambda_0}\left(v\frac{d^2(bv)}{dv^2}\right)10^2\left(1+\frac{n_{20}I}{\nabla}\right) ps/km-nm,(iii) \quad ...(3.38)$$

$$\text{where } \nabla = \frac{n_0 - n_2}{n_2} \quad ...(3.39)$$

Total Dispersion : Single Mode Fiber

In order to minimize the total dispersion of a signal through a single mode fiber, it is essential to operate it a wavelength longer than 1.37μm. At that wavelength the small value of material dispersion cancels the small wave guide dispersion. Thus, the total dispersion is reduced to zero as shown in Fig. 3.6. The Zero dispersion point occurs near 1300 nm wavelength. At this wavelength there is also a small attenuation of the signal through the fiber, this helps the operation of a data link at this wavelength. Thus a low dispersion at this wavelength gave an impetus for the development of a family of sources and receivers which will operate at this wavelength.

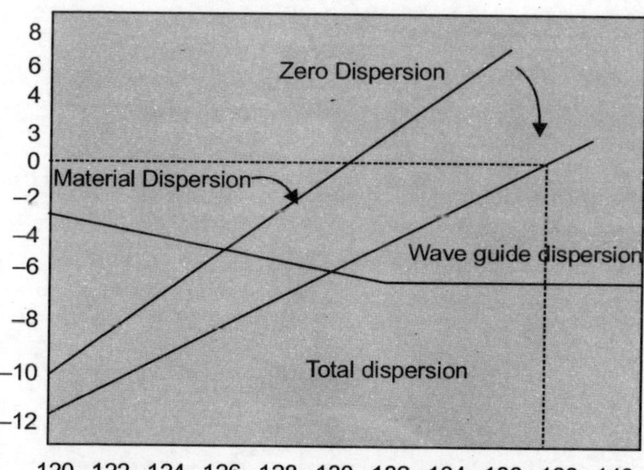

Fig. 3.6 : Addition of fiber material dispersion and wave guide dispersion of a single mode fiber to achieve zero dispersion at an wavelength of 1.37 μm

The amount of wave guide dispersion has been found to depend on the amount of doping level as well as the core radius 'a' and the refractive index gradient Δ between the core and cladding. As for the triangular doping profile (*Fig 3.6*) zero dispersion is attained at other wavelengths between 1300 nm and 1700 nm. Thus it was possible to develop fibers that have a minimum attenuation and zero dispersion at the wavelength of 1500 nm. This process is called the 'dispersion shifting' and the fiber is referred to as the 'dispersion shifted fiber'.

REFERENCES

1. John M.Senior, Optical Fiber Communications – Printice Hall International (UK) Ltd. 1992.
2. Cristani., Opt: Communn., Vol. 146, 1998
3. S.K. Turistyn and E.G. Shapiro. Opt. Lett 23, 1998.
4. K. Prozean Proc. Indian Nat. Sci Acad. 67, 2001.
5. D. Anderson Proc. Inst. Electr. Engg. Vol. 123, 1985

4

OPTIMIZATION OF DISPERSION IN OPTICAL FIBER USING SOLITONS THROUGH THE NON-LINEAR SCHRODINGER EQUATIONS (NSE)

Introduction

Optical fibers have created a revolution in the field of telecommunication and have become the backbone of today's global communication networks. Optical fiber communication is considered to be more advantageous because, it has large channel handling capacity, high signal to noise ratio due to presence of low noise, no electromagnetic interference etc. In communication engineering, optical fiber and free space communications is being more and more important. Apart from these remarkable advantages, the major disadvantages are information loss and cross talk because of optical loss and dispersion[1].

Optical time division multiplexed (OTDM) transmission system has been a topic of continuous research due to their unique advantages over conventional NRZ based transmissions, including the possibility of non-linearity based all-optical information processing, and tolerances on dispersions penalties in the link. Among various key technologies which enable the successful integration of OTDM system, high repetition rate, transform limited pulse source still remains as one of the issues that require further optimization. Still, most pulse sources developed so far had one or more drawbacks to be used as an information carrier, with unavoidable problems like timing jitter, pulse dropping, or severe chirp in the pulse, inherent in their generation methods. The recently proposed pulse shaping method using Dispersion Decreasing Fiber (DDF) resolved several past issues providing high quality pulse with exact signal timing, but the application mostly has been limited to ultra-high repetition rate above 100's GH_z[2]. The required length to generate pulse stream at low repletion rate (~10GH_z) becomes close to hundreds of km, making this approach impractical for OTDM applications[3].

To solve this problems, using fundamental soliton train with relatively short pulse width instead of sinusoidal signal at the input section of the DDF has been suggested, making the adiabatic compression scheme applicable to low repetition rate. Other method includes generation of femtosecond pulses from a short segment of DDF after a preliminary compression of higher order (N~3.5) input soliton pulse from electro-absorption modulator (EAM) in standard single mode fiber (SMF). Still, this scheme has a little disadvantage in terms of spectral purity and complexity in generating short pulses in EAM. It has been proposed a new scheme for generating a pedestal-free, femtosecond soliton pulse train from sinusoidal input signal by utilizing quasi-adiabatic pulse compression in two stage dispersion decreasing fiber, to achieve a high compression factor > 250[4].

In this analysis, it has been rather provided excessive effective amplification in the DDF so that the input sinusoidal signal could evolve into higher order soliton, instead of N=1 soliton. Although the input signal was not higher order soliton but sinusoidal. Since the output pulse evolved into a higher order soliton, a broad side pedestal was observed as can be seen in Fig 4.1. After this quasi-adiabatic pulse compression process, reduction of pulse pedestal (in terms of pulse peak power ratio) from ~ –10dB to ~30dB has been achieved with the saturable absorber, in the case of non-linear amplifying loop mirror (NALM).

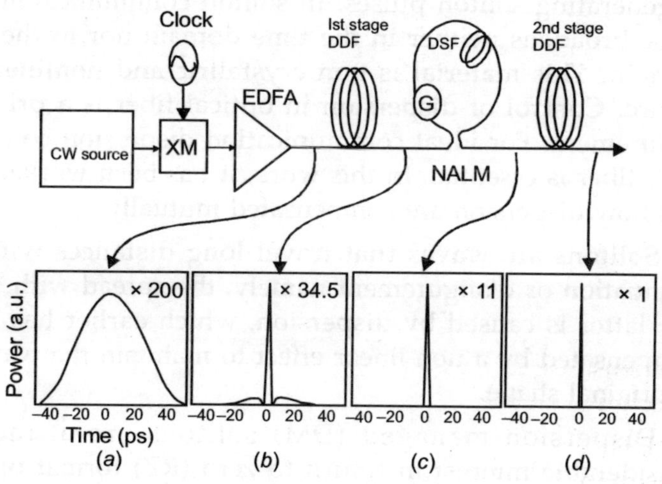

Fig. 4.1 : Schematic Diagram for pulse compression

Figure 4.1 shows the reshaped pulse train with remarkably reduced pedestals from –12.5dB to –33.dB after the NALM. The gain of amplifier and the length of DSF used in the NALM were regulated so that the NALM switching power equivalent to the peak power of pulse train coming out from the first stage DDF. It has been used the non-linear fiber loop mirror in the mid-stage of the pulse shaping process to achieve complete pedestal removal at following DDF stages. As a result of this pre-tailoring of the pedestal from the NALM, the second stage DDF, designed for conventional adiabatic fundamental order soliton compression provided much better pulse compression ratio and pedestal reduction reshaping the pulses from NALM into pedestal-free femtosecond solitons. As a result the output pulse obtained at the end of the whole evolution process, with 207fs pulse width after the transmission of second stage of DDF. The length of the DDF used in the second stage was only 500m, with the linear dispersion decreasing profile 10ps/nm/km down to 1.95ps/nm/km[5].

The problem of dispersion can be overcome with the help of generating soliton pulses. In soliton communication the pulse broadens neither in the time domain nor in the free domain. This material is non crystallric and nonlinear in nature. Control of dispersion in optical fiber is a primary requirement. For ideal communication dispersion compensator fiber is essential. In this work, it has been worked out that how dispersion are compensated mutually.

Solitons are waves that travel long distances without attenuation or disfigurement namely, the spread with time. The latter is caused by dispersion, which earlier has been compensated by a non-linear effect to maintain the wave in its original shape.

Dispersion managed (DM) solitons are attracting considerable interest in return to zero (RZ) format optical communication systems because of their superb characteristics which are not observed with conventional solitons in particular sufficiently strong period dispersion management allows for the stationary propagation of non-linear RZ pulses with finite energy when the average dispersion is close or even equal to zero.[6,7,8].

Although in-line synchronous modulation requires periodic multiplexing/demultiplexing for WDM transmission, it will enable optical regeneration with reduced cost and complexity. It has been shown experimentally, that in a DM soliton system with weak dispersion management, in-line intensity modulation (IM) can significantly improve the system performance. However, generalization of the IM technique for systems with strong dispersion management is not straightforward because of the large pulse broadening leading to bits overlapping and resulting into pattern-dependent non-linear interactions. Moreover, the excess gain required to compensate for the loss due to modulation contributes to the additional build-up of noises in the zero time slots. Therefore, for strong dispersion management, where the dominant degradation results from the intrachannel non-linear effects[9,10] a simultaneous stabilization is required of the timing and amplitude jitters of bit-carrier pulses (marks) and suppression of the growing ghost pulses and the background noise in zero time slots (spaces).

In the DM line, the efficiency of conventional modulation is significantly decreased, compared with classical soliton-based transmission system[11,12,13]. In order to recover the efficiency of the control, it has been proposed to use a periodic enhancement of system non-linearity by means of extra amplification at regeneration sites to convert the DM pulse into classical soliton.

Soliton

The term 'soliton' was introduced in the 1960's, but the scientific research of solitons had started in the 19th century when John Scott-Russell observed a large solitary wave in a canal near Edinburgh. In the days of Scott Russell, there was much debate concerning the very existence of this kind of solitary waves. Now-a-days, many model equations of non-linear phenomena are known to possess soliton solutions.

Solitions are very stable solitary waves in a solution of those equations. As the term 'soliton' suggests these solitary waves behave like 'particles'. When they are located mutually far apart, each of them is approximately a travelling wave with constant shape and velocity. As two such solitary waves get closer, they gradually deform and finally merge into a singlewave packet; this wave packet, however, soon splits into two solitary waves with the same shape and velocity before 'collision' as shown in fig. 4.2.

The stability of solitons stems from the delicate balance of 'nonlinearity' and 'dispersion' in the model equations. Non-linearity drives a solitary wave to concentrate further; dispersion is the effect to spread such a localized wave. If

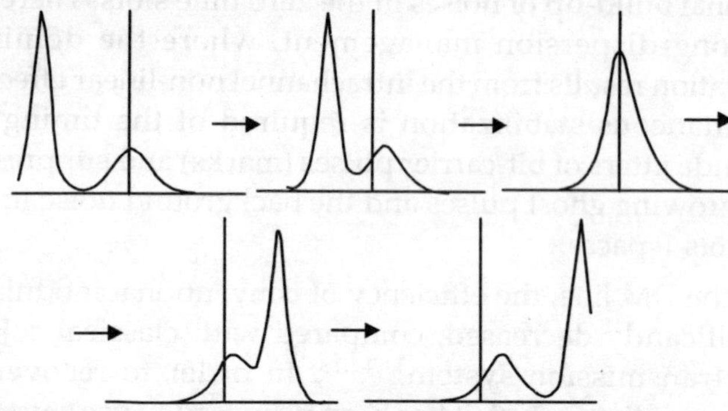

Fig. 4.2. Stable solitary waves

one of these two competing effects is lost, solitons become unstable and, eventually, cease to exist. In this respect, solitons are completely different from "linear waves" like sinusoidal waves. In fact, sinusoidal waves are rather unstable in some model equations of soliton phenomena. As shown in fig. 4.3

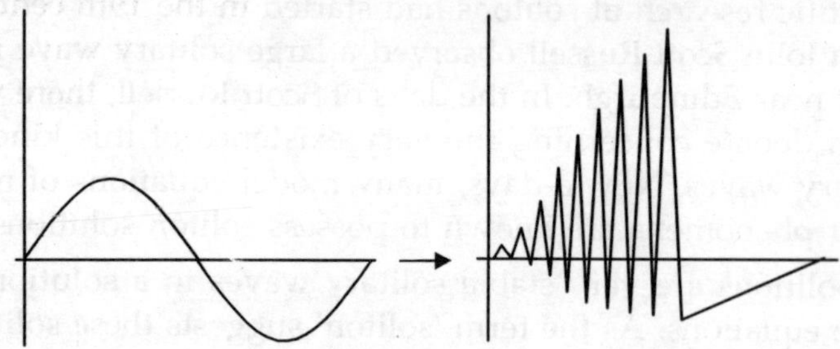

Fig. 4.3. Unstable solitary waves

The development of a simple and stable source of picosecond solitons allowed studies of the properties of these pulses in long distance transmission systems which share many characteristics with fiber lasers. A Raman amplifier which pumps a wavelength of 1545 nm was designed to provide a distributed gain for investigation of soliton properties over distances of 100 dispersion lengths. The pump source developed for the amplifier was a superfluorescent amplified spontaneous emission source capable of delivering upto

1300mW of power in a 0.5 nm bandwidth. The investigations of the behaviour of soliton pulse pairs reveals several limitations to high bit rate soliton communications over such long distances. These restrictions are caused by pulse energy fluctuations in combination with the soliton self frequency shift and the build up of dispersive radiation emitted by the solitons.

Background of the Invention

The present invention relates to a wavelength-division multiplexing (WDM) telecommunication system using dispersion-shifted optical fibers, in which noise effects due to the so-called 'Four Wave Mixing' (FWM) are avoided.

In the most recent telecommunication engineering, it is known to use optical fibers for sending optical signals of a predetermined frequency to carry information to be remotely communicated. It is also known that the optical signal sent through an optical fiber undergoes an attenuation during its travel, which necessitates amplification by means of respective amplifiers disposed at predetermined intervals along the line.

Optical amplifiers are conveniently used to achieve the required amplification. With optical amplifiers, the signal is amplified which remaining in an optical form, that it without detection and regeneration of the signal. These optical amplifiers are based on the properties of a fluoresecent dopant, such as erbium for example, which, when suitably excited by application of optical pumping energy, has a high emission in the wavelength band corresponding to the band of minimum attenuation of the light in the silica-based optical fibers.

The optical fibers used for transmission have a chromatic dispersion, which is due to the material that forms them and the refractive index profile, that varies with the wavelength of the transmitted signal and that goes to zero at a given value of the wavelength itself. This chromatic-dispersion phenomenon substantially consists of a widening in the duration of the pulses forming the signal during their travel through the fiber. This widening is due to the fact that the different chromatic components of each pulse are characterized each by its own wavelength and travel in the fiber at different speeds. Following this widening, temporarily successive pulses that are well separated at the transmitter, can partially overlap at the receiver, after their travel through the fiber. They may even be no longer distinguishable as separate values, cause an error in the reception.

Fibers of the so-called 'Step-Index' (or SI) possess such optical features that the chromatic dispersion goes to zero at a wavelength value of about 1300 nm. Therefore, SI fibers at wavelengths close to 1500nm, which is used for telecommunication, have an important value of chromatic dispersion capable of constituting a limit to the transmission speed. That is, SI fibers limit the possibility of sending a high number of successive pulses in a predetermined unit time without incurring errors at the receiver.

It is also known that the need to send increasing amounts of information over the same transmission line has led to the sending of more transmission channels over the same line by a so-called 'Wavelength Division Multiplexing' (or WDM) process. According to this technique, more channels consisting of analog or digital signals are simultaneously sent over the line consisting of a single optical fiber, and the channels are distinguished from each other in that each of them is associated with its own wavelength in the employed transmission band. This technique enables the number of the transmitted pieces of information per unit time to be increased, where the pieces of information are distributed among several channels and the transmission speed on each channel is the same.

It has been found however, that a WDM transmission through dispersion-shifted single-mode optical fibers gives rise to an intermodulation phenomenon between the channels, known as 'Four Wave Mixing' or FWM. This phenomenon arises, in general, when the presence of three optical signals in the fiber gives rise to a fourth signal which can overlap the others, thereby reducing the system performance[14]. The effect is due to non-liner third order phenomenon that can become very strong due to the high field intensity in the fiber core and at the high interaction lengths between the signals[15]. The greatest generation efficiency of the fourth wave (that is the noise effect in the system) is reduced by increasing the differences between the signal frequencies, the chromatic dispersion or the transmission length, due to the increased phase shift between the signals. In the case in which the optical fiber is a low-chromatic dispersion fiber (the above described DS fiber) and has a small efficient area of interaction between the optical frequencies (signal-mode fiber), the non-linearity resulting from generation of the fourth wave can become a limit to transmission, in that the intermodulation products can fall with in the receiving band and give rise to a noise source[16].

It is to be understood that both the foregoing general description an the following detailed description are exemplary and explanatory only and are not restrictive of the invention, as claimed. The accompanying drawings, which are incorporated in and constitute a part of this specification, illustrate several embodiments of the invention and together with the description, serve to explain the principles of the invention.

Pulse Generation by Non-linear Schrodinger Equation

The system model of the proposed idea and the pulse shapes at each stage are illustrated in figure 4.1. For the precise analysis of pulse propagation, the non-linear Schrodinger equation [NSE] was solved numerically using variation approach. It has been shown that the soliton in fiber links employing compensating fiber with variable dispersion based on the variational approach for the solution of the non-schrodinger equation (NSE) by using simple system criterion.[17]

Non-linear Schrodinger Equation [NSE]

The equation that describes the propagation of soliton pulses in periodically amplified systems with variable dispersion is:

$$i\frac{\partial u}{\partial \xi}+\frac{1}{2}d(\xi)\frac{\partial^2 u}{\partial \tau^2}+|u|^2 u = -\frac{1}{2}\Gamma+i(\sqrt{G}-1)^N\sum_{m=1}^{A}\delta(\xi-m\xi_A)u \quad ...(4.1)$$

Where N_A is the number of cascaded amplifiers, $\xi_A = Z/L_D$, $\Gamma = \alpha L_D$ is the normalized loss coefficient (α is the loss coefficient and L_D is the dispersion length), $G = exp(\Gamma\xi_A)$ is the gain provided to compensate for the losses, δ is the Dirac function, which indicates the periodic nature of the amplification, and $d(\xi)$ is the variable dispersion profile given by :

$$d(\xi) = \begin{cases} \dfrac{\beta_2^{DCF}}{\beta_2^{ave}}, \text{ for the DCF, and} \\ \dfrac{\beta_2^{DCF}}{\beta_2^{ave}}, \text{ for the DSF} \end{cases} \quad ...(4.2)$$

Where DCF and DSF stand for dispersion compensating fiber and dispersion shifted fiber, respectively, and

$$\beta_2{}^{ave} = \frac{\beta_2^{DCF}Z_{DCF}+\beta_2^{DSF}Z_{DSF}}{Z_A} \quad ...(4.3)$$

is the average dispersion coefficient.

In order to analyse the propagation of the pulse envelopes, it is convenient to write the amplitude u as a function of a fast component, due to loss and periodic amplification, and a slow component, the envelope through the transformation:

$$u(\xi, \tau) = a(\xi)\, v(\xi, \tau) \quad ...(4.4)$$

By applying this transformation to equation 4.1 the following equations are obtained :

$$i\frac{\partial u}{\partial \xi}+\frac{1}{2}d(\xi)\frac{\partial^2 u}{\partial \tau^2}+a^2(\xi)|u|^2 u = 0 \quad ...(4.5)$$

$$\frac{da}{d\xi} = -\frac{1}{2}\Gamma a+(\sqrt{G}-1)^N\sum_{n-1}^{A}\delta(\xi-m\xi_A)a \quad ...(4.6)$$

Equation 4.6 has the following solution

$$a(\xi) = \begin{cases} a_0 \exp\left(-\frac{1}{2}\Gamma(\xi - m\xi_A)\right), & \text{for } m\xi_A < \xi < (m+1)\xi_A \\ a_0 & \text{for } \xi = m\xi_A \end{cases} \quad ...(4.7)$$

with

$$a_0 = \left(\frac{\Gamma\xi_A}{1-\exp(-\Gamma\xi_A)}\right)^{1/2} \quad ...(4.8)$$

It should be noticed that, if the amplifier spacing Z_A is chosen much smaller than the dispersion length L_D. Then $\xi_A = Z_A / L_D << 1$ and $a(\xi)$ is a function of the fast variation in each interval between amplifiers. With a suitable choice of the input power, the soliton shape will deviate very little from its shape in a lossless medium and may be amplified hundreds of times with a behaviour very close to ideal propagation. The energy of the soliton in this propagation regime is the average energy in one amplification stage, and is therefore called average soliton regime.

Variation Method

Lagrangean of the System

The application of variational calculus to the solution of the nonlinear Schrodinger equation (NSE) was proposed for the first time by Anderson[18], in 1983. Since then, variational calculus has been a powerful tool in the study of soliton dynamics. It is worth noting that this method may be employed in systems with dispersion management, since the energy is conserved in average.

The differential equation that describes the optical field propagation is equation. This equation must be rewritten through variational calculus equations. The first step is to write the Euler-Lagrange equations for the system under analysis. Considering that the Lagrangean L of the system depends on the optical field and its derivatives relative to the propagation coordinate and to the temporal coordinate :

$$L\left(=L\,v,v^*,\frac{\partial v}{\partial \xi},\frac{\partial v^*}{\partial \xi},\frac{\partial v}{\partial \tau},\frac{\partial v^*}{\partial \tau}\right) \qquad ...(4.9)$$

The Euler-Lagrange equations are given by:

$$\left(\frac{\partial L}{\partial V}\right)-\left(\frac{\partial}{\partial \xi}\frac{\partial L}{\partial V_\xi}+\frac{\partial}{\partial \tau}\frac{\partial L}{\partial V_\tau}\right)=0 \qquad ...(4.10a)$$

$$\left(\frac{\partial L}{\partial V^*}\right)-\left(\frac{\partial}{\partial \xi}\frac{\partial L}{\partial C_\xi}+\frac{\partial}{\partial \tau}\frac{\partial L}{\partial V_\tau}\right)=0 \qquad ...(4.10b)$$

where $v_{\xi'}=\frac{\partial v}{\partial \xi}, v_\xi=\frac{\partial v^*}{\partial \xi}, v_t=\frac{\partial v}{\partial \tau}, v_\tau=\frac{\partial v^*}{\partial \tau}$

The Lagrangean of the system must be such that, replaced in the Euler Lagrange equations, produces the original NSE or its complex conjugate. Using this principle, the Lagrangeon of the system was found to be given by:[19]

$$L=\frac{i}{2}\left(v\frac{\partial v^*}{\partial \xi}-v^*\frac{\partial v}{\partial \xi}\right)+\frac{1}{2}d(\xi)\left|\frac{\partial v}{\partial \tau}\right|^2-\frac{1}{2}c(\xi)\,|\,v\,|^4 \qquad ...(4.11)$$

It may be easily verified that the NSE is obtained, if this Lagrangean is used in equation. It should be noted, however, that here the variable is $c(\xi) = a^2(\xi)$.

Ansatz and Average Lagrangean

Having defined the Lagrangean of the system and verified its validity through the Euler-Lagrange equations, an important step is to identify a trial function, or ansatz, which will be used as an approximation for the exact solution. The final solution, found through the variational method, is as more accurate as the ansatz is closer to the exact solution. In order to take into consideration the main system parameters that rules soliton propagation, the following ansatz was chosen.[20]

$$v(\xi,\tau) = \eta(\xi)\sec h[\eta(\xi)(\tau + \Omega(\xi)\xi \times$$

$$\exp\left(-i\Omega(\xi)\tau+i(\eta(\xi)^2-\frac{\xi}{2}+i\phi(\xi)\right) \qquad ...(4.12)$$

Where $n(\xi),\Omega(\xi,)q(\xi),\phi(\xi)$ represent the amplitude, frequency, phase and position of the soliton, respectively.

Once defined the trial function, a new calculation of the sysem Lagrangeoan is required, starting with the chosen ansatz. In this way, the Lagrangean becomes a function of the ansatz parameters.

Replacing equation (4.12) in equation 4.11, it is found that:

$$L = \eta^2 \left\{ \left(\sec h(x) - \tau \frac{\partial \Omega}{\partial \xi} + \frac{1}{2}(\eta^2 - \Omega^2) + 2\xi\eta \frac{\partial \eta}{\partial \xi} - \right) 2\xi\eta \frac{\partial \Omega}{\partial \xi} \right.$$

$$\left. + \frac{\partial \phi}{\partial \xi} + \frac{i}{4} d(\xi)(\Omega^2 + \eta^2 \tan h(x)^2 - \frac{i}{4} c(\xi)\eta^2 \sec h(x)^2 \right\} \quad \text{...(4.13)}$$

where $x = \eta(\tau + \Omega\xi - q)$.

The variational principles establishes that:

$$\delta \iint L d\xi d\tau = 0 \quad \text{...(4.14)}$$

It is possible to reduce the variational principle to only one dimension, by integrating the Lagrangean over all time τ. For this it is useful to define the reduced or average Lagrangeaon, given by.

$$\langle L \rangle = \int L d\tau \quad \text{...(4.15)}$$

Using equation (4.13), the following average Lagrangean is obtained.

$$\langle L \rangle = -2q \frac{\partial \Omega}{\partial \xi} + 2\Omega\xi \frac{\partial \Omega}{\partial \xi} + \eta^3 - \eta\Omega^2 + 2\xi\eta^2 \frac{\partial \eta}{\partial \xi} - 2\xi\eta^2 \frac{\partial \Omega}{\partial \xi}$$

$$+ \eta \frac{\partial \phi}{\partial \xi} + \frac{i}{2} \eta d(\xi)\Omega^2 + \frac{2}{3}\eta^3 - \frac{i}{3}\eta^3 c(\xi) \quad \text{...(4.16)}$$

The variational principle is then replaced by the reduced variational principle, expressed by :

$$\delta \int \langle L \rangle d\xi = 0 \quad \text{...(4.17)}$$

Ansatz Parameters

The reduced Lagrangean defines a Hamiltonian system with finite dimension. Therefore, the equations that describes the anasatz parameters can be obtained from the canonical Hamilton equations, given by:

$$\frac{dx_j}{dz} = \frac{\partial H}{\partial p_j} \quad \text{...(4.18)}$$

$$\frac{dp_i}{dz} = \frac{\partial H}{\partial x_j} \quad \text{...(4.19)}$$

Where the generalized system momentum, *p*, and the system Hamiltonian, *H*, for the reduced problem, are given respectively by:

$$p_j = \frac{\partial \langle L \rangle}{\partial \left(\frac{\partial x_j}{dz} \right)} \quad \text{...(4.20)}$$

$$H = \sum_{J=1}^{N} pj \frac{dx_j}{dz} - \langle L \rangle \quad \text{...(4.21)}$$

The generalized coordinate x_j are those that, in the reduced Lagrangean, have derivative relative to z. In the case under analysis, $z = \xi$ and the generalized coordinates of the problem are $x_j = \Omega, \eta, \phi$, for $j = 1, 2, 3$, Therefore :

$$p_1 = \frac{\partial \langle L \rangle}{\partial \left(\frac{d\Omega}{d\xi} \right)} = -2q + 2\Omega\xi - 2\xi\eta^2 \quad \text{...(4.22)}$$

$$p_2 = \frac{\partial \langle L \rangle}{\partial \left(\frac{d\eta}{d\xi} \right)} = 2\xi\eta^2 \quad \text{...(4.23)}$$

$$p_3 = \frac{\partial \langle L \rangle}{\partial \left(\frac{d\phi}{d\xi} \right)} = \eta \quad \text{...(4.24)}$$

Using equation (4.21) the following Hamiltonian is found:

$$H = \eta\Omega^2 - \eta^3 - \frac{2}{3}\eta^3 - \frac{i}{2}n\Omega^2 d(\xi) + \frac{i}{3}\eta^3 c(\xi) \quad \text{...(4.25)}$$

Using this in the Hamilton equations (4.18, 4.19), we obtain:

$$\frac{d\Omega}{d\xi} = \frac{\partial H}{\partial(-2q + 2\Omega\eta - 2\xi\Omega^2)} \Rightarrow \frac{d\Omega}{d\xi} = 0 \Rightarrow \Omega = \Omega_0 \quad ...(4.26)$$

$$\frac{dq}{d\xi} + \xi\frac{d\Omega}{d\eta} + \Omega - \eta^2 - 2\xi\eta\frac{d\eta}{d\xi} + \eta\Omega - \frac{i}{2}\eta\Omega d(\xi) = 0 \quad ...(4.27)$$

$$\frac{d\phi}{d\xi} = \frac{\partial H}{\partial\xi} \Rightarrow \frac{d\phi}{d\xi} = -3\eta^2 + \Omega^2 - \frac{i}{2}\Omega^2 d(\xi) - 2\eta^2 + i\eta^2 c(\xi)$$

$$...(4.28)$$

$$\frac{d\eta}{d\xi} = \frac{\partial H}{\partial\phi} \Rightarrow \frac{d\eta}{d\xi} = 0 \Rightarrow \eta = \eta_0 = \text{const.} \quad ...(4.29)$$

$$\frac{d\eta}{d\xi} = \frac{\partial H}{\partial(2\xi\eta^2)} \Rightarrow \frac{d\eta}{d\xi} = 0 \Rightarrow \eta = \eta_0 = \text{const.} \quad ...(4.30)$$

$$\frac{d(2\xi\eta^2)}{d\xi} = \frac{\partial H}{\partial\xi} \Rightarrow -3\eta^2 + \Omega^2 - \frac{i}{2}d(\xi)\Omega^2 - i\eta^2 c(\xi) = 0 \quad ...(4.31)$$

Equation (4.27) may now be rewritten using equation (4.26)

$$\frac{dq}{d\xi} = \Omega - \eta^2 + \eta\Omega - \frac{i}{2}\eta\Omega d(\xi) \quad ...(4.32)$$

the parameters for the soliton parameters are

$$\frac{dq}{d\xi} = 0 \Rightarrow \eta = \eta_0 = \text{const.} \quad ...(4.33)$$

$$\frac{d\Omega}{d\xi} = 0 \Rightarrow \Omega = \Omega_0 = \text{const.} \quad ...(4.34)$$

$$\frac{d\Omega}{d\xi} = -2\eta^2 0 \quad ...(4.35)$$

$$\frac{dq}{d\xi} = \Omega_0 - \eta_0^2 + \eta_0\Omega_0 - \frac{i}{2}\eta_0\Omega_0 d(\xi) \quad ...(4.36)$$

From these results it may be concluded that, for this type of propagation :

- The amplitude of the envelope of the slow variation function is constant.
- The soliton frequency is constant.
- The phase varies linearly with propagation distance.

The NSE was solved with the variational approach, with a general ansatz of the type[19]

$$U(z, t) = (A(z)ft)/B(z) \exp [iP(z) + iC(z)t^2] \qquad ...(4.37)$$

Where $A(z)$, $B(z)$, $P(z)$ and $C(z)$ account for the complex amplitude, pulse width, phase and pulse chirp, respectively. By applying the variational principle, the NSE reduces to a set of ordinary differential equations:

$$A(z)^2 B(z) = \text{const.} \qquad ...(4.38)$$

$$\frac{dB}{dz} = 2d(z)BC \qquad ...(4.39)$$

$$\frac{dC}{dz} = \frac{d(z)K_1}{2B^4} - \frac{C(z)A^2K_2}{B^2} - 2d(z)C^2 \qquad ...(4.40)$$

Where K_1 and K_2 are constants that depend on the shape of input pulse, For sech pulse, $K_1 = 2K_2 = 4/\pi^2$.

Optimization of Dispersion

The dispersion compensation scheme is reported where the uniform DCF is replaced by fiber with decreasing and increasing dispersion profiles. In this study, three cases were considered for the dispersion coefficient of the compensating fiber: uniform (conventional DCF), exponential decreasing, and exponential increasing. In order to do a fair comparison as general as possible, the average dispersion of the dispersion-varying compensating fiber (DVCF) was set to be equal to the dispersion of the uniform fiber[21].

Result and Discussion

In one aspect, the analytic method presents invention relates to an optical telecommunication system having at least two sources of optical signals modulates at different wavelengths, included in a predetermined transmission wavelength band, at a predetermined transmission speed; means for multiplexing said signals for input to a single comprising optical fiber; and optical-fiber line connected at one end to said multiplexing means; and means for receiving said signals comprising optical demultiplexing means for the signals themselves depending on the respective wavelength.

The signals have no optical power of a value greater than a predetermined value in at least one portion of the optical-fiber line, which line comprises an optical fiber line, which line comprises dispersion value lower than a predetermined value in said transmission wavelength band. The optical fiber has a chromatic dispersion that increases with the wavelength increase, exhibiting a zero value at a wavelength lower than the minimum wavelength of the band by such an amount that no local zero value of chromatic dispersion present in the fiber and capable of generating a four-wave-mixing phenomenon is included in the band.

In particular, the wavelength value bringing the chromatic dispersion to zero is lower by at least 10 nm than the minimum wavelength to the transmission band. Preferentially, the wavelength value bringing the chromatic-dispersion to zero is lower than or equal to 1520 nm and, more preferably, the chromatic dispersion value in the fiber is lower than 3 ps/(nm.km) in the predetermined transmission band. Also preferably, the predetermined optical power value in at least one portion of the line is not lower than 2 mW per channel.

In a particular embodiment, a system consistent with the invention comprises at least one optical amplifier interposed along the optical line. In particular embodiment, the system comprises at least four optical amplifier has a signal-amplifying band comprising the predetermined wavelength band and, preferentially, the signal amplifying band is included between 1530 and 1570 nm. In a particular embodiment, the system comprises at least four optical amplifiers.

In a second aspect, the invention relates to an optical fiber for transmitting at least two optical signals in a predetermined transmission wavelength value included in a predetermined interval. The maximum zero for a wavelength value included in predetermined interval. The maximum value of the interval is lower than the minimum wavelength of the band by such an amount that substantially no local wavelength value bringing the local chromatic dispersion to zero include in the band, but which is present in the fiber over a length portion capable of generating intermodulation peaks of said signals. In particular, each of the wavelength zero values of the local chromatic dispersion differs by less than 10 nm from the wavelength zero value of the overall chromatic dispersion in the fiber. Also in particular, the optical fiber according to the invention has a chromatic dispersion lower than 3 ps (nm.km) in the transmission band, and it becomes zero for a transmission value lower by at least 10 nm than the minimum wavelength value of the band.

In another aspect, the optical fiber consistent with the invention is characterized in that, for an overall fiber length greater than 100-km, it has a chromatic dispersion of such a value that intermodulation peaks are not generated in the presence of at least two optical signals over several channels of different wavelengths, the power of which being at least 3 mW per channel fed to a fiber end, and the intensity of which causing a signal/noise ratio lower than 20.

In a further aspect, the invention relates to a process for transmitting optical signals at a predetermined transmission speed, including the steps of generating at least two modulated optical signals of predetermined wavelengths included in a predetermined transmission band, the wavelengths being different from each other by at least 2 nm, feeding said signals to a single-mode optical fiber having a chromatic dispersion lower than 3 ps/(nm.km) in the transmission band and a zero point of the chromatic dispersion at a predetermined wavelength, amplifying the optical signal at least once by at least one optical active-fiber amplifier, transmitting said signals over a distance of at least 50 km, and receiving said signal through a demultiplexiing receiver. The minimum wavelength value of the transmission band is higher by a given amount than the wavelength value bringing the chromatic dispersion to zero, which amounts to have such a value that in no efficient fiber portion the chromatic value in the band becomes zero. Preferentially, the minimum wavelength of the transmission band is higher than the zero value of the chromatic dispersion by at least 10 nm. More preferentially, the wavelength value brining the chromatic dispersion to zero is included between 1500 and 1520 nm. Preferably, the predetermined transmission speed is higher than or equal to 2.5 Gbit/s.

According to a further aspect, the invention concerns an optical fiber for transmitting optical signals to non-linear phenomena in a predetermined transmission wavelength band, characterized in that it has a chromatic dispersion lower than a predetermined value in the band and which becomes zero for a wavelength value included in a predermined interval, the maximum value of which is lower than the minimum wavelength of the band by which is present in the fiber over a length portion capable of generating spectral modification of said signals. Preferably, each of the wavelength zero values of the local chromatic dispersion differs by less than 10 nm from the wavelength zero value of the overall chromatic dispersion in the fiber.

In particular, the optical fiber has a chromatic dispersion lower than 3 ps/(nm.km) in the transmission band, which becomes zero for a wavelength lower by at least 10 nm than the minimum wavelength value of the band. Preferably, the predetermined transmission wavelength band ranges from 1530 to 1560 nm.

In material dispersion for silica, at wavelength 1550 nm, with dispersion obtained is 22 ps/km-nm. Whereas in waveguide dispersion process for the same wavelength in silica the dispersion obtained is 22 ps/km-nm. In general it has been observed that the dispersion is optical fiber is equal to 1.6dB for distance of 11-km. In the second aspect the dispersion is 0.8 db/km in the Rayleigh Scattering process where the wavelength of the source is 1×10^{-6}m at a temperature of 140^0 K. In another aspect the dispersion is 0.5 dB/km when the wavelength is equal to 1.3μm in the stimulated Raman Scattering process where as in the silica silica glass and germanium doped silica glass the dispersion 0.1dB/km when the wavelength of the source is 1.2 μm which is not possible in practical but can be achieved theoretically.

An analytic theory describing the equal for nearly equal spacing of pulses in harmonic passively mode-locked depletion of the gain across the soliton pulse causes a group-velocity drift proportional to the spacing between pulses. An analytic model capturing the effect of the time dependant gain on the pulses by including a phenomenological perturbation to the nonlinear Schrodinger equation have been developed.

Dispersion-Managed (DM) optical data transmission has become a mainstream in the development of high speed communication systems. DM soliton systems have significant advantages over classical soliton transmission lines: enhanced energy, resulting in higher signal to noise ratio (SNRs), reduced timing jitter, and strongly reduced non-linear mixing between wavelength-division-multiplexed (WDM) signals. Single channel 40-GB's transmission over 10000-km has also been reported in a DM line composed of dispersion-shifted fiber (DSF) and dispersion compensation fiber (DCF). However, in 40 Gb/s systems with strong dispersion management as in links based on standard fiber (SMF), DM return-to-zero(RZ) transmission is limited by intrachannel non-linear effects and corresponding intersymbol interference (ISI).

The transmission fiber of 50-km length is either DSF with dispersion $d = 1$ ps/km/nm, dispersion slope $d'' = 0.06$ ps/nm_2/km, loss $\alpha = 0.21$ dB/km, and effective area $A_{eff} = 55$ μm^2, or SMF with $d = 17$ ps/km/nm, $d'' = 0.06$ ps/nm^2/km, $\alpha = 0.21$ dB/km, and A_{eff}=26 ps/nm/km, d″ = –0.2 ps/nm^2/km, $\alpha = 0.5$ dB/km, and $A_{eff} = 26$ μm^2. The length of DCF is adjusted to provide residual dispersion around zero. As non-linear fiber, we considered the HNF with $d = 1.8$ ps/nm/km, $d'' = 0.03$ ps/nm^2/km, = 0.5 dB/km, and non-linear coefficient

n_2/A_{eff}=2 × 10 – $^{-9}W^{-1}$. The erbium-doped fiber amplifier (EDFA) with a nose figure of 6 dB is installed after the DCF for both systems.

We first apply stability analysis to the DM line with a weak map strength operating at 10 Gb/s and 40 Gb/s in order to validate the accuracy of the stability analysis for different transmission regimes. Here, the DSF is used as a transmission fiber; the average dispersion is 0.05 ps/nm/km, and the pulse energy is 0.15 pj.

First numerical results demonstrating 40-GB/s transmission over 20000-km of SMF using modified modulation technique have been reported in 6H8. However, comprehensive investigation of the stable regimes in multidimensional parameter space is limited by the computational time required for a single optimization run. New effective approaches are then highly desirable for further system optimization. The combined action of the filters, modulators.

Figure 4.1(a~b) shows the 10GHz sinusoidal input signal at 21 dBm average power evolving into the compressed pulse train with 1.76ps full width at half maximum (FWHM) pulse. The first DDF has the total length of 13.6-km and linearly decreasing dispersion profile, from 10ps/nm/km at the input to 3.2ps/nm/km at the output. Note that the length of the first DDF is much shorter than that of a DDF required in Mamshev's analysis, where the sinusoidal input evolves into a fundamental soliton.

Conclusion

Dispersion-Managed (DM) optical data transmission has become a mainstream in the development of high speed communication systems. DM soliton systems have significant advantages over classical soliton transmission lines: enhanced energy, resulting in higher signal to noise ratio (SNRs), reduced timing jitter, and strongly reduced non-linear mixing between wavelength-division-multiplexed (WDM) signals.

The system model of the proposed idea and the pulse shapes at each stage are illustrated for the precise analysis of pulse propagation, the non-linear Schrodinger equation [NSE] was solved numerically using variation approach. It has been shown that the soliton in fiber links employing compensating fiber with variable dispersion suggesting the possibility of an optimal dispersion compensating profile for soliton transmission in a periodically amplified system. Here it is proposed to find an optimal dispersion based on the variational approach for the solution of the non-schrodinger equation (NSE) by using simple system criterion.

In this work it is concluded that dispersion in optical fiber is 0.21dB/km for an effective area of d = 1ps/km/nm and as the length of DCF is adjusted to reduced dispersion around zero.

In non-linear fiber the dispersion can be reduced to 0.5db/km by adjusting the length of DCF.

From these results it is further stated that, for this type of propagation, the amplitude of the envelope of the slow variation function is constant, the soliton frequency is constant the phase varies linearly with propagation distance.

REFERENCES

1. G.P. Agarwal, Non-linear Fiber Optics – San Diego, Calit Academic.
2. Pavel V Mamyshev, Stainlar V.Chernikor and E.M. Dianov Quntum Electron Vol. 27 (1991).
3. Chernikov, S.V. Guy, M.J. Taylor, J.R. Moodie, D.G. and Kashyap, R. Opt lett. Vol. 20 ,1995.
4. M.D. Pelusi, Y. Matsui and A.Suzuki., Electron Lett. Vol. 35, 1999.
5. Duckey Lee, Hosung Yoon and Namkyoo Park CLEO'99 September Paper FAI, 1999.
6. J. Nagel, 'Fiber Issues for System Development' in PWC Optical Fiber Communting, 2001.
7. N.J. Smith, F.M.Knok, N.J.Dovan, K.J.Blow and I.Bennian – Electrons Lett. Vol. 32, 1996.

8. M. Suzuki, I. Mortia, N. Edagawa, S. Yamamoto, H. Taga and S.Akiba–Electron Lett. Vol. 31, 1995.
9. I. Morita, K. Janaka, N. Edagawa and M. Suzuki, in Proc. Eur. Conf. Optical Communation, Madrid, Spain,1998.
10. P.V. Mamyshev and N.A. Mamysheva – Optical Lett-Vol. 24,1999.
11. R.J. Essiambre, B. Mikkelsen and G. Raybon-Electron lett. Vol. 35, 1999.
12. B. Dany, P. Brindel, O. Leclerc and E. Desurvive Electron lett., Vol. 35., 1999.
13. B. Dany P. Brindel, E. Pincemiv, D. Rouvillian and O. Leclerc – Opt.lett-2000.
14. Journal of LightWave Technology, Vol. 8, No. 9, 1990.
15. Journal of LightWave Technology, Vol. 10, 1992.
16. Journal of LightWave Technology, Vol.1, 1993.
17. A. Hasegawaand, Y. Kodama, 'Soliton in Optical Communication', Clarendon Press, Oxford, 1995.
18. D. Anderson 'Variational Approach to Non-linear Pulse Propagation in Optical Fibers', Phy. Rev. A. Vol. 27, 1983.
19. Ildar Gabitor, Elena G., Shapiro and Segei K. Turitsyn, 'Optical Pulsev Dynamics in Fiber Links with Dispersion Compensation', opt.comm. Vol. No. 134, 1997.
20. G. P. Agrawal 'Fiber Optics Communication System' John Willey & Sons, Newyork, 1997.
21. Alessandro. M. Melo, M.C. Gouveia and Herique. J. A. desilva 'Advance in Communication and Software Technologies', WSEAS Press, 2002.

5

APPLICATIONS OF SOLITON FOR THE FEATURE NETWORK

Introduction

The first recorded solitary wave was observed in the 1834 when a young engineer named John Scott Russell was hired for a summer job to investigate how to improve the efficiency of designs for barges that were designated to ply canals particularly the Union Canal near Edinburgh, Scotland. One August day, the tow rope that was connecting the mules to the barge broke and the barge suddenly stopped but the mass of water in front of its blunt prow rolled forward with great velocity, assuming the form of a large solitary elevation, a rounded, smooth and well defined heap of water, which continued its course along the channel without change of form or diminution of speed. "Russell pursued this serendipitous observation and followed it on horseback, and overtook it still rolling on at a rate of some eight or nine miles per hour, preserving its original form some thirty feet long and a foot to a foot and a half in height." He then conducted controlled laboratory experiments using a wave tank and quantified the phenomenon in an 1844 publication. He demonstrated four facts:

1. The solitary waves that he observed had a hyperbolic secant shape.
2. A sufficiently large initial mass of water can produce two or more independent near-solitary waves that separate in time.
3. Solitary waves can cross each other 'without change of any kind'.
4. In a shallow water channel of height h, a solitary wave of amplitude A travels at a speed of $[g(A + h)]^{1/2}$, where g is the gravitational acceleration. That is, larger-amplitude waves move faster than smaller ones—a non-linear effect.

In 1895, Dutch physicist Diederick Korteweg and his student Gustav de Vries (KdV) derived a non-linear partial differential equation (PDE),

$$\phi_t + \phi_{xxx} + 6\phi\phi_x = 0, \qquad \text{...(1)}$$

that now bears their name. Korteweg and de Vries argued that the KdV equation (1) could describe Russell's experiments. Equation (1) shows that the rate of change of the wave's height in time is governed by the sum of two terms: a non-linear one (the amplitude effect) and a dispersive one (the effect that causes waves of different wavelengths to travel with different velocities). Korteweg and de Vries found a periodic solution in addition to a solitary-wave solution that resembled the wave that Russell had followed. These solutions arose as a result of a balance between non-linearity and dispersion. Their work and Russell's observations fell into obscurity and were ignored by mathematicians, physicists, and engineers studying water waves until 1965 when Norman Zabusky and Martin Kruskal published their numerical solutions of the KdV equation (and invented the term 'soliton'). Kruskal derived (1) as an asymptotic (continuum) description of oscillations of unidirectional waves propagating on the 'cubic' Fermi-Pasta-Ulam (FPU) non-linear lattice. Meanwhile, Morikazu Toda became the first to discover a soliton in a discrete, integrable system.

In a 1967 , Zabusky and Gary Deem showed numerically that a modified KdV equation also exhibits soliton-like interactions (Fig. 5.1) Robert Miura recognized the significance of this result and found an exact transformation between this

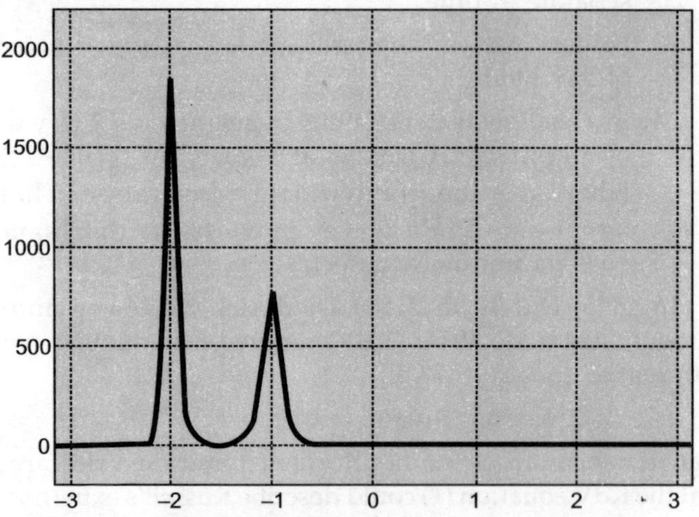

Fig. 5.1 : Collision between two soliton solutions of the KdV equation

modified KdV equation and equation (1). This awakened the mathematical study of solitons, as Clifford Gardner, John Greene, Martin Kruskal, and Robert Miura in 1967 were able to solve the initial-value problem for the KdV equation by introducing the *inverse scattering method*, providing an appropriate notion of *integrability* for continuum frameworks. Vladimir Zakharov and Alexei Borisovich Shabat generalized the inverse scattering method in 1972 when they solved the non-linear Schrödinger (NLS) equation, another model non-linear PDE, demonstrating both its integrability and the existence of soliton solutions. In 1973, Mark Ablowitz, David Kaup, Alan Newell, and Harvey Segur demonstrated the existence of soliton solutions of several other non-linear PDEs, including the sine-Gordon equation. Other researchers have subsequently derived other integrable PDEs and constructed accompanying soliton solutions. As the Kadomtsev-

Petviashvili (KP) equation illustrates, one needs to be more nuanced as to what constitutes a 'soliton' in multiple spatial/ dimensions. When studying solitary waves in non-integrable equations, analytical techniques typically rely on perturbative methods, asymptotic analysis, and/or variational approximations. An important example of a non-integrable system with exact solutions for isolated solitary waves are the coupled mode equations for fiber Bragg gratings in optics.

Research on solitary waves and solitons remains one of the most vibrant areas of mathematics and physics. It has had a broad and far-reaching impact in myriad fields ranging from the purest mathematics to experimental science. This has led to crucial results in integrable systems, non-linear dynamics, optics, biophysics, super symmetry, and more.

Little could attendants to John Tyndall's lecture at the Royat Society of London in 1870 imagine that the simple experience they were witnessing in which Tyndall showed how the usual straight line paths followed by light rays could actually bend down to follow a stream of water flowing through a hole in a illuminated vessel, would ultimately set the scientific basis over which the today's, more than a hundred years later, information highways and hence the whole concept of life and society is built up. The experience endowed with scientific category the phenomenon of interdielectrics light guidance very lilcely already familiar to Grecian and other ancient glassblowers who could have used it in fabricating their decorative glassware. As a matter of fact, some of the techniques used by the old Venetian glassblowers for making 'millifiore' have provided useful hints for the building up of the present fiber optics industry. A rigorous theoretical description of the phenomenon, by Hondros and Debye, tooli still forty years to appear and still 17 years more were needed to find any practica1 application.

A crude assembly of fibers to demonstrate the basic image and light transmission properties of fibers. Before the great success attained by rnicrowave, technology as applied to remote sensing and both free space and guided transmission, some theoretical studies that praised the great possibilities that optical carriers could offer, as greater transmission bandwidths, greater angular resolution and greater Doppler shift for moving target detection[1], were passed over. Fiber optics applications pointed therefore at a different direction. By the 30's the medicine industry already benefited from light piping around corners that allowed illurnination of the hidden, of great utility for example in gastroscopy. However, since uncoated fibers were used, the efficiency was low, whereupon these ideas were not actively pursued and lay dormant until the early 1950s when Van Heel in Holland and Hopkins and Kapany in the UK reactivated the field with the basic purpose of developing an efficient 'flexible fiberscope'. From this renowned interest van Heel's idea of using solid coatings of lower refractive index to improve the light transmission efficiency was born giving rise to a burst of research activity for whose designation Kapany coined the today's familiar name of *Fiber* Optics. Even though irnage transmission through bunches of fibers (which were fabricated following similar techniques to those employed in Palestine to produce glass mosaics in the first century B.C.) was considered thus paving the path for application of fiber optics to transmission, by that time al1 the applications of fiber always concerned guidance of incoherent light with power losses in the 1000dB/km range. However amazing it may sound today, when the appearance of the laser in 1960 provided a powerful coherent source for modulation and transmission, the ñrst optical transmission thoughts were for free space optics and complex systems were designed often using huge lens as repeaters[2]. Driven by the development of the transistor in 1947, the 60's are as well the years of the digital revolution: in the telephony network, the 64 kbps voice channels were progressively introduced, and in 1969 ARPANET, a network connecting computers at 56 kbauds began to operate. Better quality and variety of new services drove an exponential increase in the demand for connectivity that led to great congestion both in the radioelectric spectrum and in the cities underground ducts housing thick wire cables. The marlet demand for telecommunications services seemed to have overcome the possibilities offered by the microwave technology which together with the network maintenance problems mainly derived from the high failure rate of repeaters required every 2-km, spurred the search for new transmission techniques and solutions.

After 10 years of research efforts devoted to find the link between optics and transmission, the Corning Glass Worlrs came about with the answer: following the suggestion of Haus, H. and W. S. Wong[3] the losses in the fiber were lowered down to 20dB-km in the same year when room operation of a semiconductor laser was made possible. Optical transmission began to be considered an alternative to copper wires and the first fiber optics transmission links were constructed around 1973 which used LEDs or GaAlAs lasers and a carrier wavelength of X *N* 850nm for which the silica features a minirnum losses spectral window with attenuations in the 4dB-km range.

Optical systems entered the telephony networli through intercity link, i.e., the trunli telephony networli, in the third voice channel multiplexing hierarchy comprising 64 voice channels and data rates around 34Mbps. Existing technology by that time did not allow the fabrication of very thin fibers which would only permit one transmission mode and hence the repeaterless transmission length was severely limited by intermodal dispersion to about 10-km. Single mode fibers were made possible by 1976 and together with improvement of light sources and detectors, a new generation of optical transmission systems was born, called the second generation (which of course assumed the previous systems to belong to the, first generation) working in the X *N* l.3 pm minimum losses spectral window with losses in the O. 5dB-km. These systerns could carry third hierarchy streams (34Mbps) with repeater distances of 50-km, or fourth hierarchy (140 Mbps, 256 voice channels) with 15-20 km between repeaters. Still a third generation born around 1979, uses the third spectral window X *N* 1.5 pm with losses around 0.2dB-km and data rates around 565 Mbps, comprising about 1024 voice channels, and typical repeaterless distances of 50 Km.

Today the replacement of electronic repeaters which required the subsequent previous optical-electronic and ulterior electronic-optical transformations by optical Erbium Doped Fiber Amplifiers (EDFA) fed through laser diodes, as providing a fully optical point-to-point link through which any bit stream can be transmitted regardless of its data format, velocity or carrier wavelength, has added versatility to the system which in addition results more reliable due to the reduction in components. That further allows with traditional NRZ format, dispersion-shifted fibers and other techniques designed to compensate for dispersion, to increase the channel capacity in commercial optical links up to about 10 ~ b pasn d 10.000-km of repeaterless distance. With the use of EDFAs, multiplication of the channel capacity through the use of several carrier wavelengths, the so-called Wavelength Division Multiplexing (WDM) technique, is econornically feasible. As allowing accumulation of nonlinear effects along the link, EDFAs further open the door to *soliton* based transmission. Concerning fiber transmission, optical solitons designate these pulses arising from an interplay between linear dispersion and the nonlinearity present in the fibre which due to its very special properties can propagate over very large distances without significant alteration of its temporal profile. One may say that when solitonic propagation takes place the linear dispersion is compensated through the non-linearity[4].

In front of traditional NRZ format and linear dispersion-compensation, whose technologies already well-lcnown and established, soliton-based RZ formats as taking advantage of the non-linearities present in the system, not only remove the need for non-linearity compensation techniques, but offer in addition bit unit robustness against perturbations and a suitable format for performing temporal switching.

Accustomed to the theoretically simpler basic principles of operation of linear systems, the technology world is quite reluctant to introduce non-linear systems into the market but ultimately 'money talks' and most likely the technology which proves more reliable and cheap while offering greater capacity will prevail. Through the use of WDM it has been demonstrated in field experiments that the bit velocity and distance at which existing technology is capable of sending information over the optical fibre are not likely to be exceeded by the telecommunications market requirements. Specifically *lTbps (100Gbps x10* WDM channels) transmission over a *40-km* fiber loop has been reported[5]. Another issue is handling and routing of this information which still has to be done by electronic means ensuing data format change in every switching node which reduces the performance. If the increas-ing demand for a growing variety of telecommunications systems is to be satisfied, techniques that allow to remove this 'electronic bottleneck' as it is often referred, and pave the path to a future *All-optieal Global N ~ ~ U J O T* in~, which not necessarily all parts in the network rely on optical technology, but the information travelling in the network has always optical format, both for transrnission and routing, need to be searched for.

About the same year that the first operative fiber transmission systems were deployed, Hasegawa predicted that short enough optical pulses in the subpico second regime at the wavelengths for anomalous dispersion should propagate in the fiber as *optical solitons*[6]. The word soliton alludes to the particle-like properties of certain localized structures which propagate undistorted over long distances thanks to the non-linear compensation of linear effects such as dispersion or diffraction, and undergo elastic collisions[7]. Chance provided the first observation of such structures in the form of water waves in a Scottish narrow barge channel in 1838. J. Scott Russell's report in 'Reports of the Meetings of the British Association for the Advancement of Science' in 1844 talks about 'a large solitary elevation, a rounded, smooth and well defined heap of water, which continued its course along the channel, apparently without change of form or diminution of speed' and which emerged in the channel when a boat suddenly stopped. The mathematical formulation of the phenomenon is owed to Korteweg and deVries who in 1895 published their famous KdV equation. Zabusky and Kruskal in 1965 rediscovered the phenomenon numerically and were the first to use the word soliton. Starting from Zabusky and Kruskal's studies the analytic theory leading to formulation of the inverse scattering method for mapping the non-linear solution to the KdV on solutions of a linear system of equations was developed by Gardner et al.[8]. In 1972,[9] Zakharov and Shabat showed that the nonlinear Schrodinger equation describing intense pulse propagation in a fiber supports solitons that can be derived using inverse scattering theory at the same time of Hasegawa prediction[10], Observation of optical solitons had to wait development of an appropriate laser which could provide short enough pulses at the wavelength of anomalous dispersion in the fiber, around 16 A ~ 1.5-km, a task that was covered by L.P. Mollenauer and co-workers at the Bell Laboratories so that they finally could experimentally observe optical soliton propagation in a fiber by 1980[11]. With the advent of the EDFA, the idea of using solitons as the bit unit for long distance optical transmission began to take shape. Key field demonstrations of the feasibility of this idea were performed by L. F. Mollenauer, at Bell Laboratories. At the same place and almost at the same time, M. N. Islam and co-workers demonstrated the soliton dragging and soliton trapping properties of biréfringent fibers allowing for the switching and routing of data streams in the temporal domain . Just as the same way that optical solitons in the temporal domain manage to preserve their shape on propagation through the power dependent non-linear phase shift compensating linear dispersion, *spatial solitons* may be formed from non-linear compensation of diffraction so that the spatial beam distribution remains unaltered on propagation. Spatial solitons were observed for the first time by Y. Silberberg and G.I. Stegeman[12] in a planar waveguide made of liquid C8% by 1985, while their excitation in a solid-state waveguide was achieved, once again, at Bell Laboratories by Atchinson et al.[13]. These spatially localized structures might be convenient for the design of spatial routers and other switching devices but for a third order non-linearity only are stable in the 1+1 case, namely monochromatic wave propagation in planar waveguides.

Solitons

A solitary wave is a localized 'wave of translation' that arises from a balance between non-linear and dispersive effects. In most types of solitary waves, the pulse width depends on the amplitude. A *soliton* is a solitary wave that behaves like a 'particle', in that it satisfies the following conditions. It must maintain its shape when it moves at constant speed.

1. When a soliton interacts with another soliton, it emerges from the 'collision' unchanged except possibly for a phase shift.

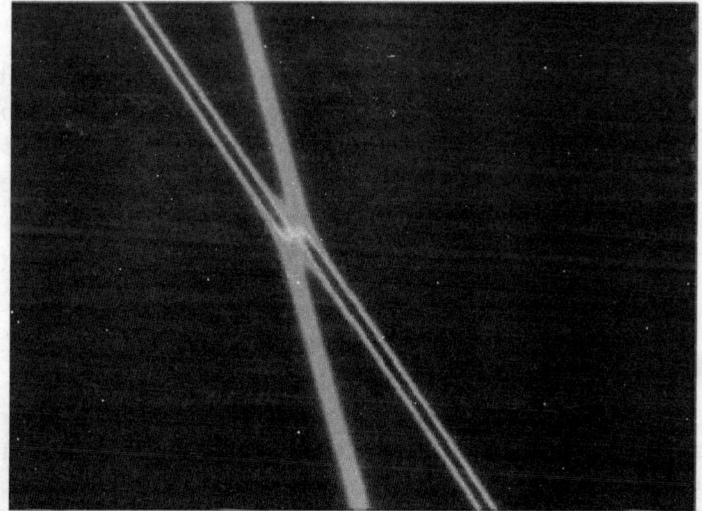

Fig. 5.2 : Space-time diagram of the collision

That is, for a conservative (non-dissipative) system, a soliton is a solitary wave whose amplitude, shape, and velocity are conserved after a collision with another soliton (*Fig. 5.2*). We provide code that is set up to show the collision between two soliton solutions of the Korteweg-de Vries (KdV) equation. In the physics literature, the terms 'soliton' and 'solitary wave' are often used interchangeably. Solitary waves (and solitons) arise in both continuous systems such as the KdV equation and discrete systems such as the Toda lattice and in both one and multiple spatial dimensions. Key issues in studying solitary waves also include linear versus non-linear (of course), integrable versus non-integrable, persistent versus transient, asymptotics (i.e., consideration of time scales), localization in physical space versus Fourier space, and the effects of noise.

Although it seems that solitons are now sometimes taken for granted, they are in fact very special objects. Without the benefit of hindsight, it is absolutely amazing that solitons exist at all. One might have expected nonlinearity to destroy such structures, particularly in light of decades of experience with low-dimensional non-linear dynamical systems.

- Many physical systems can be modelled quite successfully using equations that admit soliton solutions. Indeed, solitons and solitary waves have been observed in numerous situations and often dominate long-time behaviour.
- Equations with soliton solutions have a profound mathematical structure.

Stability of Solitons

The most remarkable fact is actually not the possibility of the mentioned balance of dispersion and non-linearity, but rather that soliton solutions of the non-linear wave equation are very stable: even for substantial deviations of the initial pulse from the exact soliton solution, the pulse automatically 'finds' the correct soliton shape while shedding some of its energy into a so-called dispersive wave, a weak background which has too little intensity to experience significant non-linear effects and temporally broadens as a result of dispersion. Solitons are also very stable against changes of the properties of the medium, provided that these changes occur over distances which are long compared with the so-called *soliton period* (defined as the propagation distance in which the constant phase delay is $n/4$). This means that solitons can adiabatically adapt their shape to slowly varying parameters of the medium. Also, solitons can accommodate to some amount of higher-order dispersion; they then automatically adjust their shape to achieve the mentioned balance under the given conditions.

Higher-order Solitons

If the pulse energy is the square of an integer number times the fundamental soliton energy, the pulse is a so-called *higher-order soliton*(*Fig. 5.3*). Such pulses do not have a preserved

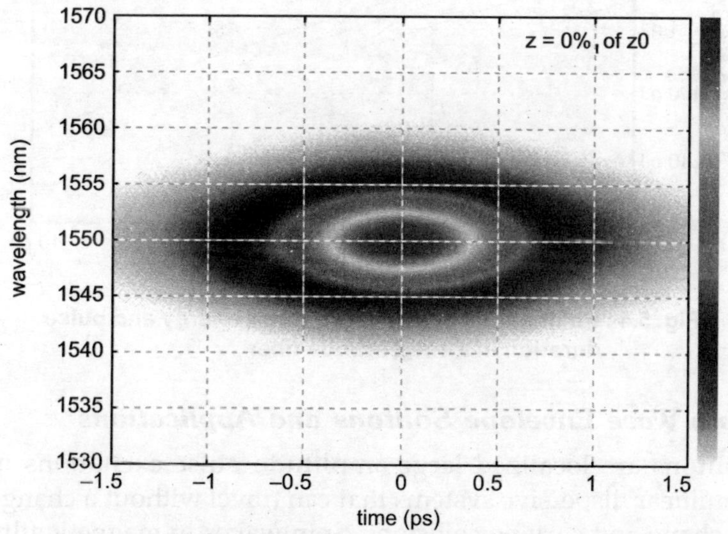

Fig. 5.3 : This animated spectrogram shows how a third-order soliton evolves in a fiber

shape, but their shape varies periodically, with the period being the above-mentioned soliton period. Higher-order solitons can break up into fundamental solitons under the influence of higher-order dispersion and other disturbing effects. They are by far not as stable as fundamental solitons.

Importance of Solitons

Fundamental soliton pulses are technically very important, in particular for long-distance optical fiber communications and in mode-locked lasers. In the latter situation, soliton-like pulses can be formed when the typically lumped pieces of dispersion and nonlinearity in the laser cavity are sufficiently weak. Solitons are also applied in various techniques for pulse compression using optical fibers; examples are adiabatic soliton compression and higher-order soliton compression (Fig. 5.4).

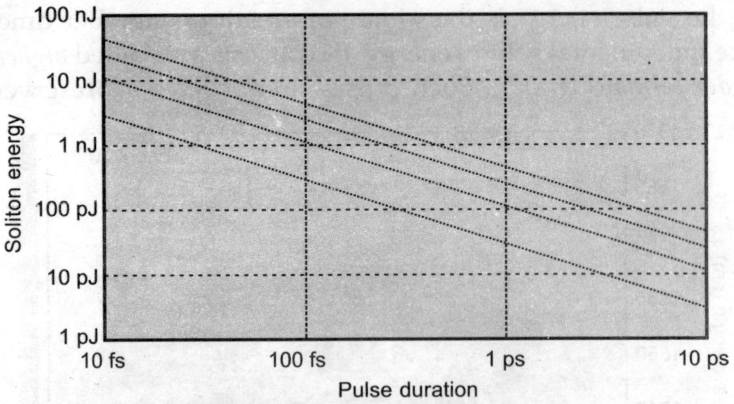

Fig. 5.4 : Relation between soliton pulse energy and pulse duration in a single-mode fiber

Spin Wave Envelope Solitons and Applications

Solitons are localized large-amplitude pulse excitations in nonlinear dispersive systems that can travel without a change in shape and survive collisions. Spin waves in magnetic film systems provide a powerful and versatile 'test bed' for the study of fundamental soliton dynamics. Taking the advantage of the spin waves, we discovered many intriguing phenomena involving solitons, including soliton fractals in feedback rings, exact and periodic Fermi-Pasta-Ulam (FPU) recurrence, random formation of coherent solitons from incoherent waves, soliton formation through coupled modulational instability, and the formation of dark solitons through spontaneous modulational instability (*Fig. 5.5*).

Fig. 5.5 : Large-amplitude pulse excitations

Magnetic Millimeter Wave Devices

Microwave magnetic devices have had a major impact on the development of microwave technology (*Fig. 5.6*). At present, there is a critical need for the extension of current microwave magnetic device physics and technology into the millimeter (mm) wave range. This need is critical for two reasons: (1) Millimeter waves are recognized as a broadband frequency resource for wireless links; (2) Electromagnetic radiation at mm-wave frequencies can penetrate clouds, fog, and many kinds of smoke, all of which are generally opaque to infrared or visible *light*.

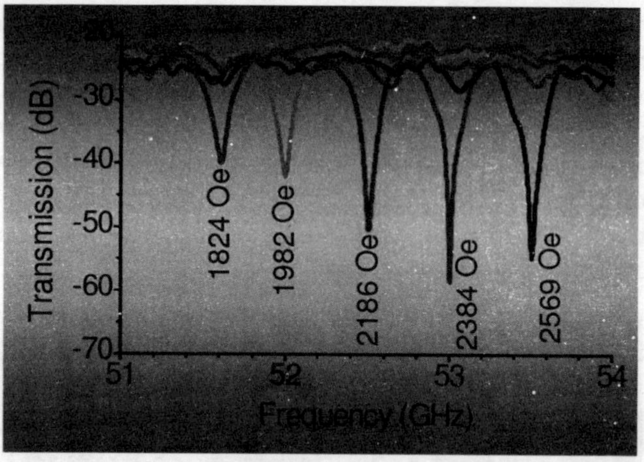

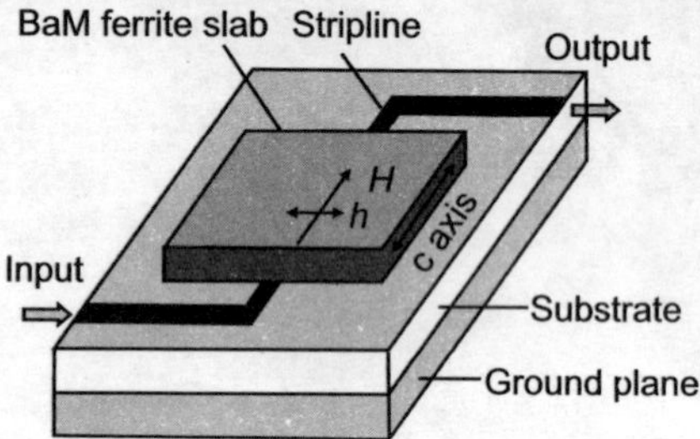

Fig. 5.6 : Microwave magnetic device

Microwave-assisted Magnetization Reversal

In the presence of microwaves, magnetization reversal or switching in magnetic materials can take place at significantly reduced switching fields. This effect is called microwave-assisted magnetization reversal (MAMR) (*Fig. 5.7*). The physical mechanism of this effect is that a microwave magnetic field can excite large-angle magnetization precessions which can serve to reduce the magnetic field needed for the magnetization to switch. The MAMR effect has potential applications in high-density hard disks, magnetic random access memory, and microwave devices. We have demonstrated the MAMR responses in a number of different magnetic elements, including Permalloy nano dots and large-damping FeCo thin films.

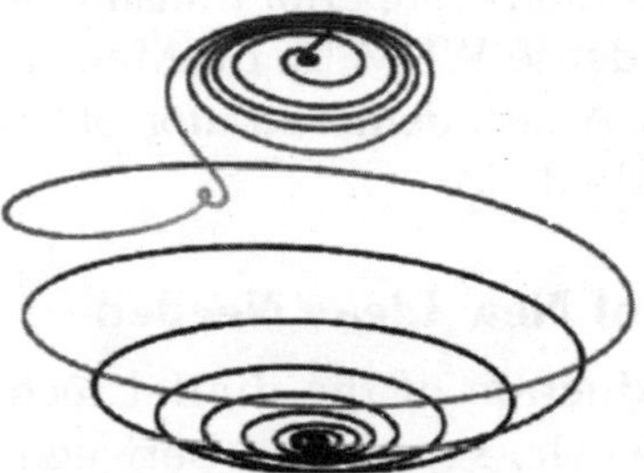

Fig. 5.7 : Magnetization reversal

Latest Issues of Soliton

Despite the remarkable success of DMSs, there remain a number of unsolved problems, one of them is their application to dense WDM systems. In dense WDM systems, in order to maximize the bandwidth efficiency, a large number of channels are packed into a limited band-width. It has been found that DMSs could be destroyed if channel spacing were too narrow. In addition, when two solitons at neighbouring channels overlap in time at the input, large temporal position shifts results. An other unsolved problem is that of polarization mode dispersion (PMD). In optical fibers, the degeneracy of two orthogonal polarizations is generally broken down because these two polarization states generally have different propagation characteristics. As a result the NLSE becomes a coupled equation that represents the two polarizations having two different group velocities and dispersions. Simulation results based on the numerical solution of these coupled equation have shown that the soliton pulse should broaden and its broadening is proportional to the square-root of distance z. The challenge for the soliton community is to demonstrate the merit of soliton for a WDM system. This could be achieved through the reduction of non-linear cross-talk either by means of a strong local dispersion, by densely managed dispersion, by a doubly periodic dispersion management, or by taking advantage of the intrinsic nature of a soliton. In this regard the recent experimental demonstration of superior transmission quality of high order DMSs in dense WDM by du Mouza et. al.[14] deserves special attention. A clear demonstration of DMSs withstanding PMD is also desired.

The Prospect of New Ideas Needed

With the introduction of the digital technology into the telephony networlc, separation between voice and data networks no longer made any sense. Since all information had the same format in transmission it was not such a crazy idea to join all telecommunication services in a unique transmission network which would merely act as a data conveyor so that only emittei and receiver nodes would need to know the nature of the data for human interpretation while the rest of switching nodes would route and process the data regardless of the service they belonged to. That is the idea behind the Integrated Services Data Network, IDSN, standard developed by the mid 70's and designed to constitute the basis of a *Global Network* that would gather all communication services in a unique plug.

Whether the great capacity offered by optical fibers has spurred the increase in the connectivity demand and with it, supported by the flexibility of the digital format, the urge for creation of new telecommunication services and facilities, or whether the degree of development achieved by optical transmission industry precisely responds to this growing necessity for connectivity, the truth is that presently telecommunication services have become an essential ingredient in our everyday life. That is so to the point that it is being said that after the two great revolutions that marked radical changes in the Human Society concept, namely the Agricultura1 and the Industrial Revolutions, the third great radical change is being determined by the possibilities offered by telecornmunications in what is called the *Information Era.*

Certainly, telecommunication services are at the very basis of our society, hereof the importante of disposing of a reliable network that handles all the traveling information in an efficient and safe manner. Before the foreseen great demand for telecommunication services and the feasibility of data transrnission over the fiber at lOGbps data rates and beyond, the fixed 64Kbps per channel defined by the ISDN standard appear ridiculous and evidence the necessity of new architectures and concepts for the Global Network management, The new Broadband ISDN standard designed for a better exploitation of the fiber optics bandwidth, considers flexible bandwidth channels in which every user occupies only the bandwidth that its transrnission requires in every moment which is also the one for which he is charged for. To that aim, the standard foresees the use of Asynchronous Transfer Mode (ATM) with packet switching and establishment of virtual connections that may be shared by pacltets belonging to different services and different virtual connections. When these brilliant ideas are to be put into practice, one should consider that significant amounts of pacltets need to be routed throughout the network without significant delays noticeable to the user. To that aim, huge switching centers made out of ultrafast switchers capable of massive parallel switching are to be required . Electronic switches based on VLSI technology are cheap and reliable and are believed to be able achieve switching velocities up to 40 Gbps or so but when arranged in large centers of bit processing, experience a significant reduction in performance due to the parasitic capacitances of connections. There is in addition the network transparency issue. Shifting to electronics entails interpretation of the packet in every switching node which kills the flexibility sustained by the BISDN standard. Packet switching and routing regardless of the pacltet meaning or the service it belongs to is therefore only achieved if the same data format is used for routing and transrnission[15]. Design and building up of devices capable of optical data switching and routing is one of the goals pursued by the *Photonics Technology* which at present is vigorously developed at a research level and holds the potential of large switching velocities and large parallel arrangements inherent to photonic processes.

Finding the Right Soliton for Future Networks

European researchers say their study of self-sustaining solitary light wave packets could result in a new generation of computers and optical telecommunications networks. Using light rather than electronic or magnetic devices to store and move data is quicker, more energy efficient and cost-effective, and cavity solitons could be the key to unlocking this technology.

A soliton is defined as a wave, which once formed, maintains its shape while it travels at constant speed. Soliton waves are localised within a region and are able to react with other solitons and emerge unchanged. This is in contrast to normal waves that diffuse over time over ever larger regions of space, a phenomenon called dispersion. Solitons were first documented in 1834 by John Scott Russell who, quite by chance, observed the phenomenon in a canal in Scotland where soliton waves formed in water. He was able to reproduce this phenomenon in a water tank. It was not until the 1970s that scientists suggested optical solitons could exist in optical fibres. In the late 1980s French and Belgian scientists were able to transmit soliton pulses over a fibre-optic cable. Since then there has been an increasing amount of research into solitons and their practical applications for the rapid transmission of data over long distances.

Prospect of Exciting Applications

The scientists believed there were properties unique to cavity solitons that could give rise to applications more advanced than what is possible using today's technology. For instance, such solitons have the extraordinary property that they can be formed and destroyed – 'written and erased' – at the micrometer scale in such a cavity. The project has gone a long way toward advancing that theory. The properties of cavity solitons are particularly applicable to the developing scientific fields of photonics and optoelectronics, which aim to use light as a method of storing, manipulating and transmitting data. The science could ultimately result in a new generation of computers and optical networks.

Optoelectronics employs the electrical effects of materials on light. The FUNFACS researchers first sought to demonstrate the viability of self-sustained cavity soliton lasers (CSL), both as continuous waves and as pulsed waves that can be switched on and off. They worked from the premise that since a soliton in an optical fibre is self-sustaining once it has been created, a cavity soliton is similarly self-sustaining within its cavity after its creation. Lasers (light amplification by stimulated emission of radiation) consist of a gain medium inside a highly reflective optical cavity. The gain medium, which can be solid, liquid or gas, is the major determining factor of the wavelength of operation, and other properties, of the laser. The cavity is coupled to an energy supply directed to the gain medium. In the case of a CSL the gain medium is the semiconducting material. The test CSL was based on an existing semiconductor laser type known as a vertical-cavity surface-emitting laser (VCSEL) which is used in a variety of applications, including those relating to optical telecommunications. The device consists of a thin optical cavity sandwiched between two highly reflective mirrors, fabricated out of solid semiconducting material using state-of-the-art nanotechnology.

An All-optical Future

The researchers were able to show that due to the self-sustaining properties of cavity solitons the energy input required to maintain them is small. They were also able to show CSLs can be switched on and off using light pulses. The research results indicate that CSLs could play an important role in an all-optical telecommunications system, according to project coordinator Robert Kuszelewicz. "In conventional systems data are switched and routed within the network by converting light pulses into electrical signals and back again which slows down communications and creates a lot of waste heat," he says. "But by using CSLs the switching can be done just with the light pulses with no need to convert to and from electricity thus giving much greater transmission speed and efficiency."

The discoveries could lead to an evolution from the current use of chip-based semiconductors for data processing to a more flexible type of optical processing. The advantages of optical processing stem from the way data is stored. Once data has been imprinted on a semiconductor chip, its location is permanently fixed, while data held using cavity soliton technology can be moved without changing or losing its character. However, Kuszelewicz believes such a breakthrough is still a long way in the future. The first practical applications could be in hybrid semiconductors using current technology coupled with optoelectronic technology based on cavity solitons. He also points out the two technologies each have their own strengths and drawbacks and will continue to exist alongside each other for a long time to come.

On the Verge of a New Generation of Optical Devices

Presently, both market requirements and technology maturity have reached the point where alloptical operation in the networlr is cost-effective and therefore after over 30 years of preparations, the time seems to have come for all-optical devices to reach their place in the network[16]. Throughout these years the all-optical concept itself has experienced changes which responded to the telecommunications market evolution, optical materials industry development and the possibilities and impossibilities progressively found by basic phenomena research. Thus, from the initial all-optical concept as totally opposed to electronics entailing an almost complete elimination of all electronic parts in the network, the concept has evolved to approach eventual practical realizations to be equivalent to *Network Transparency,* meaning that even t hough many parts of the network may benefit from the advantages offered by electronics, the data format is always optical, so that from a combination of optics and electronics, a more efficient network management is accomplished. Other changes in the all-optical devices research mentality concern optical materials technology. A material with strong enough third-order non-linear response and low losses which can bring into reality the many theoretical studies about all-optical switching in waveguides has yet to be discovered. Only fiber based devices which take advantage of the accumulated non-linear phase shift over long propagated distances thus providing low-power temporal all-optical switcking operation feature some chances of entering the commercial marltet even though still their technology is not mature enough so to allow for mass production. Second-order non-linear materials on their side, whose technology, due in great part to the electrooptical external laser modulators industry development, has reached a high degree of maturity presently are in a good position to constitilte an alternative for some future all-optical devices. This is so specially for the ubiquitous Lithium Niobate, *LiNbOs,* to the point that its key role in optical technology is somehow compared to that of silicon for the electronics industry, although significant irnprovements coming from intensive research are still required to approach switching performance marltet requirements. Another of the drives of the all-optical devices research change of mentality is the telecommunications services marltet incredible grow which has led to the conviction that in the near future all-optical networlt operation will become necessary to respond to the demand for connectivity, At present, the existing options which have been considered for all-optical operation deployment do not appear still as definitive ones and hence till the time when the telecommunications demand urges for all-optical network management, new ideas and solutions need to be searched for. Since all-optical light control with applicability to switching and routing operation is based on non-linear optical processes, the new ideas should come through vigorous research in the Nonlinear Optics research field.

Non-linear Optics Research : From Intriguing Phenomena to Useful Applications

Non-linear effects in light propagation were identified as early as 1875 when J. Kerr observed double light refraction in an isotropic liquid which had quadratic dependence upon the incident field. Another double refraction effect but with linear dependence upon the incident field was observed later on, in 1906, by F. Pockels in several crystals. Although some applications of these non-linear effects, named after their discoverers Kerr and Pockels effects respectively, were envisioned[17], for any practical realization to be considered seriously a reliable enough, stable, powerful light source was required. The new light source developed by 1960, the laser, came to meet all these and still more requirements allowing for construction of both Kerr and Pockels cells which served as high speed optical modulators, and optical frequency doublers, among others. The avalanche of new discoveries made possible with the advent of the laser gave birth to a new research activity field taken to be called generically *Non-linear Optics*. Non-linear Optics applications have been traditionally divided into two main research areas. On one side there were the processes involving more than one frequency, such as optical modulation and rectification and frequency doubling, mainly relying on second-order phenomena, i.e. the polarization depends of the square of the electric field. On the other side, third order processes in which the polarization depends on the electric field to the cube so that the non-linear field contribution has the same frequency as the input resulting in a net non-linear phase shift experienced by the input field as a consequence of the material's non-linearity[18]. This power dependent non-linear phase shift was meant to taken advantage of for all-optical switching in interferometric devices and directional couplers, and in general for functions related to handling and processing of information for the sake of more efficient telecommuni-cations networks management. While the results in the first research activity have moved to the commercial arena, so that efficient external laser modulators relying on the electrooptic or Pockels effect and laser frequency doublers were ready to meet the market requirements in practical applications, the second research field was mainly developed at a theoretical level due to the lack of suitable materials with strong enough third order non-linear response free from absorptive losses which would allow for obtention of the required non-linear phase shift. When, by 1990, it seemed that the lack of suitable materials with a high enough third order non-linearity might have led the topic of all-optical switching by exploitation of nonlinear phase shifts to a stand by status, large phase shifts steaming from a second-order non-linearity in Potassium Titanil Phosphate were observed by DeSalvo and co-workers at the Center for Research and Education in Optics and Lasers, CREOL[19]. This observation opened a new field for exploration which was generically known as *Cascading.* Although their relevance was not fully acknowledged at the time, phase shifts in excess of *TT* had already been observed by Khaykovich.L, et al.[20] in organic CDA. The phase distortion effect occurring in second harmonic generation processes had been indeed a matter of concern but merely as a limiting factor of the efficiency of frequency doublers, being not identified as a new way to achieve all-optical operation. As a matter of fact, the existence and relevance of the %(2) induced non-linear phase shift, was recognized as early as 1967 by E.A. Ostrovskaya[21] although at that time the idea was not actively pursued due to the lack of suitable materials.

The non-linear phase mismatch in second-order processes is the result of the contribution to the incident field at fundamental frequency of consecutive up-conversion to second harmonic and down-conversion back to fundamental processes in such a way that it is proportional to the input field intensity |£^o| and the square power of the corresponding non-linear coefficient, here of the name of Cascading. Significant phase shifts in short propagated distances with moderate power levels are therefore achieved thanks to stronger x non-linear response of existing materials.

Waveguide structures confine the light beam in very small regions allowing to reach high power levels that thus improve the non-linear phase shift and ease integration. The first experiments demonstrating the x non-linear phase shift in a waveguide were carried out again at CREOL in KTP samples and Lithium Niobate structures by A. Desyatnikov and co-workers[22]. The effect has been demonstrated in a wide variety of materials: 3-barium borate, potassium niobate, semi-conductors such as gallium arsenide, orgànics as MBA-NP, DAN, NPP and D AST. Some of the cited materials exhibit impressively huge non-linear responses that hold promise for applications provided long enough, lowloss samples can be fabricated in geometries where the appropriate elements of the x tensor are used. To the significant phase shift observations at CREOL, suggestioned for its use in all-optical devices. With these discoveries, second-order non-linear processes, till 1990 only thought useful for frequency doubling and optical modulation via the electrooptic (Pockels) turned out to be promising as well for the practical realization of some all-optical switching devices.

Solitons in Non-linear Quadratic Structures

If the non-linear phase shift is the effect balancing linear dispersion/diffraction for temporal/spatial soliton formation in third-order non-linear media, can the non-linear phase shift induced through a second-order non-linearity under some conditions achieve as well the equilibrium so that a solitary entity made up of fundamental and second harmonic waves propagating together is formed? Some clues as to a positive answer can be adduced. On one side there is the fact that under some conditions the coupled normalized equations governing the propagation of first and second harmonic beams reduce to the Non-linear Schrôdinger Equation which is known to support exact solitary wave solutions, and on the other one has the existence of an analytic solitary wave solution to the normalized equations for certain fixed values of all parameters in the system. This solution is seen to constitute a mere sample of a broader family of stationary solutions whose transverse profiles can not be cast into analytic form. Although the potential of second-order non-linear processes to support solitonic propagation was recognized as early as 1974 by Yu.S. Kivshar[23], it was not until the boom of cascading in the 90s that the possibility of obtaining steady solitary waves structures in quadratic non-linear media aroused the curiosity of the scientific community and along with new findings some of the earlier results were rediscovered. The numerical experiments simulating propagation in x media evidenced the existence of solitary wave structures made up of fundamental and second harmonic beams propagating locked together and emerging from a wide variety of input and system conditions. These solitary wave structures featured an oscillating behavior around stationary states. They were shown to be actually the ones around which the solitary wave structures slightly oscillated in the simulations and their stability confirmed through several theoretical works. In addition to single solitary waves, multihumped solutions were also shown to verify the stationary equations but in all cases presented to date they turned out to be unstable. Besides being excited with significantly lower power levels, the new x solitons were found to be stable not only in 1 + 1 arrangements as the old-known x solitons were, but also in 2 + 1 and 3 + 1 structures thus opening the door to two dimensional routing of bits and to the practical realization of *light bullets.* Modulational instabilities of (1 + 1) and (2 + 1) solitons yielding (3 + 1) bullets have also been examined.

Towards a Transparent Network

Optical technology is now dominant in long haul communications networks and globally transports >50% of all traffic.

The new optical devices and transmission systems now emerging offer revolutionary network options that could eclipse all previous operational gains. Specifically, coherent optics will allow very high traffic densities per fibre and optical amplifiers offer the possibility of full network transparency. Future long haul networks are thus likely to require far less hardware and control, but will offer a far greater utility and reliability than at present.

Coherent Optical Systems: Current Status and Future Prospects

The purpose of this chapter is to review the current status of coherent systems for point-to-point and network applications. The review covers components, subsystems and systems and concludes with an outline of the future prospects.

Laser Phase-noise Reduction in a Self-homodyne Optical Link

Laser phase noise manifests itself as a degradation in SNR or BER in coherent optical communication systems. Real systems, particularly those employing phase modulation, often require sub-megahertz linewidth sources to perform satisfactorily. Experimental laboratory systems offer greater flexibility in their realisation and in this paper a novel technique is described to reduce the effective linewidth of semiconductor lasers, which is appropriate to such laboratory experiments.

Fibre Optic Connectors with High-return-loss Performance

This chapter describes the development of a single mode fibre optic connector with high return loss performance without the use of index matching. Partial reflection of incident light at a fibre optic connector interface is a recognised problem where the result can be increased noise and waveform distortion. This is particularly important for video transmission in subscriber networks which requires a high signal to noise ratio. A number of methods can be used to improve the return loss. The method described here uses a process which angles the connector endfaces. Measurements show typical return losses of –55dB can be achieved for an end angle of 6 degrees. Insertion loss results are also presented.

Simple Homodyne Technique for the Characterisation of Wideband Optical Detectors

The behaviour of solitons in optical fibres has been an area of study for some time. The interest in this rather fascinating field of non-linear phenomena has varied from initially modest to the current interest in the possibility of a new type of data communication system. This paper will set out, in an non-mathematical way, the properties of these optical solitons. The type of soliton that will be considered is the envelope soliton, which consists of a carrier wave with a (complex) envelope that is modulated.

Generation of Periodic Sequence of Solitons Without Pedestal for Optical Telecommunication Systems

Fast-acting telecommunication systems based on optical solitons will require, for information encoding, the high repetition rate sequential pulses, which can be produced with the aid of induced modulational instability. The disadvantage of the method consists in the accompanying generation of wide pedestal, resulting in the nonlinear interaction between pulses and information losses. The results of our numerical investigations have shown that an employment of the induced Raman effect can suppress it. A sharp increase in contrast (by an order of magnitude) and irregular character of residual background lead to significant depression of sequential pulses interaction. Stability of such pulses generation as well as optimum conditions are discussed in the present work.

Explicit Construction of the KdV Soliton

It is illustrative to demonstrate the construction of the soliton solution of the KdV equation (1) explicitly. We start with the ansatz

$$\phi = \psi(y), y = x - Ut, \qquad ...(2)$$

which describes a wave translating with speed U. Inserting this into (1) yields

$$-U\psi' + \psi''' + 6\psi\psi' = 0 \qquad ...(3)$$

where $l \equiv \frac{d}{dy}$. Integrating (3) and then multiplying the resulting equation by ψ' and integrating again yields

$$-\frac{U}{2}\psi^2 + \frac{1}{2}(\psi')^2 + \psi^3 + G_1\psi + G_2 = 0,$$

where G_1 and G_2 are constants of integration.

We want a solution in the form of a localized pulse, so we need ψ, ψ', and all higher derivatives to vanish as $y \to \pm\infty$. This implies that $G_1 = G_2 = 0$. [If one keeps non-zero constants, one can instead derive extended waves in the form of elliptic functions. This gives

$$-\frac{U}{2}\psi^2 + \frac{1}{2}(\psi')^2 + \psi^3 = 0 \qquad ...(4)$$

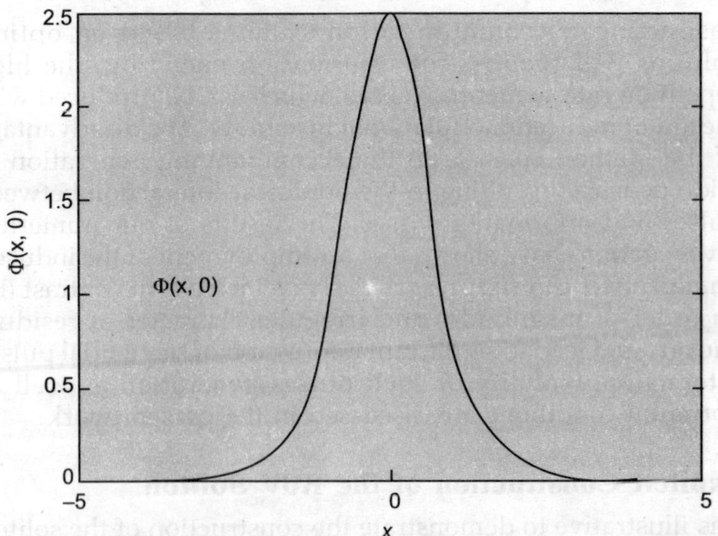

Fig. 5.8 : The wave $\phi(x, t)$ in equation (5) with $U = 5$, $x_0 = 0$, and $t = 0$.

Solving (4) by separation of variables yields

$$\phi(x, t) = \frac{2}{2}\sec h^2\left\{\frac{\sqrt{U}}{2}(x - Ut - x_0\right\}, \quad \text{...(5)}$$

where x_0 is a constant. We depict the solution (5) in (*Fig. 5.8*).

The Solitary Wave Menagerie

Since the discovery of solitary waves and solitons, a menagerie of localized pulses has been investigated in both one dimension and multiple spatial dimensions, though one must be nuanced when considering what constitutes a solitary wave (or even a localized solution) in multiple spatial dimensions. Many localized pulses have been given a moniker ending in 'on' for conciseness, although they do not in general have similar interaction properties as solitons. The most prominent examples include the following :

Envelope Solitons

Solitary-wave descriptions of the envelopes of waves, such as those that arise from the propagation of modulated plane waves in a dispersive non-linear medium with an amplitude-dependent dispersion relation. One typically uses the descriptor *bright* to describe solitary waves whose peak intensity is larger than the background (reflecting applications in optics) and the descriptor *dark* to describe solitary waves with lower intensity than the background.

Solitary Waves with Discontinuous Derivatives

Examples of such solitary waves include compactons, which have finite (compact) support, and *peakons*, whose peaks have a discontinuous first derivative. There have also been studies of cuspons which have a singularity in the first derivative rather than simply a discontinuity.

Gap Solitons

Solitary waves that occur in finite gaps in the spectrum of continuous systems. For example, gap solitons have been studied rather thoroughly in NLS equations with spatially periodic potentials and have been observed experimentally in the context of both nonlinear optics and Bose-Einstein condensation.

Intrinsic Localized Modes (ILMs)

ILMs, or discrete breathers, are extremely spatially-localized, time-periodic, stable or very long-lived excitations in spatially extended, discrete, periodic systems. (At present, it is not clear whether analogous time-quasiperiodic solutions can be constructed for general lattice equations.) ILMs, which are localized in real space, arise in a large variety of non-linear lattice models and are typically independent of the number of spatial dimensions of the lattice, the size of the lattice (which is, however, assumed to be large), and (for the most part) the precise choice of non-linear forces acting on the lattice. The mechanism that permits the existence of ILMs has been understood theoretically for more than a decade, and such waves have now been observed in a wide variety of physical systems.

υ-breathers

Exact time-periodic solutions of spatially extended non-linear systems that are continued from the normal modes of a corresponding linear system. In contrast to ILMs, *υ*-breathers are localized in normal-mode (Fourier) space, so that almost all of the energy is locked into a single Fourier mode for all time. (The label *υ* refers to the wave number of the normal mode.) They also provide the best-known explanation for FPU recurrences.

Topological Solitons

Solitons, such as some solutions to the sine-Gordon equation, that emerge because of topological constraints. One example is a *skyrmion*, which is the solitary-wave solution of a nuclear model whose topological charge is the baryon number. Other examples include *domain walls*, which refer to interfaces that separate distinct regions of order and which form spontaneously when a discrete symmetry (such as time-reversal symmetry) is broken, *screw dislocations* in crystalline lattices, and the *magnetic monopole*. One-dimensional topological solitons are necessarily kinks, which we discuss below.

Kinks

The only one-dimensional topological solitary wave, it represents a twist in the value of a solution and causes a transition from one value to another. Kinks can sometimes be represented using heteroclinic orbits, whereas pulse-like solitary waves can sometimes be represented using homoclinic orbits. Kinks are sometimes used to represent domain walls.

Vortex Solitons

A term often applied to phenomena such as *vortex rings* (a moving, rotating, toroidal object) and *vortex lines* (which are always tangent to the local vorticity). Coherent vortex-like structures also arise in dissipative systems.

Dissipative Solitons

Stable localized structures that arise in spatially extended dissipative systems. They are often studied in the context of non-linear reaction-diffusion systems.

Oscillons

A localized standing wave that arises in granular and other dissipative media that results from, e.g., the vertical vibration of a plate topped by a layer of free particles.

Higher-Dimensional Solitary Waves

Solitary waves and other localized (and partially localized) structures have also been studied in higher-dimensional settings. One example of a genuine two-dimensional soliton is the 'lump' solution of the KP equation of the first type (i.e., the KP1 equation). This type of soliton decays algebraically rather than exponentially and is sometimes described as 'weakly localized'. The KP1 equation also has unstable *line soliton* solutions (a generalization of the soliton solutions of the KdV equation), which decay exponentially in all but a finite number of directions. The KP equation of the second type (i.e., the KP2 equation) differs from the KP1 equation in that it has the opposite sign in front of its diffusion term. The KP2 equation has stable line-soliton solutions, which (unlike line solitons in the KP1 equation) can merge with each other to form a single line soliton (which can, in turn, disintegrate into two separate line solitons).

Numerous generalizations of the above examples have also been investigated, as one can consider chains of solitons, discrete analogs of the above examples (such as discrete vortex solitons), semi-discrete examples (such as spatiotemporal solitary waves in arrays of optical fibers), one type of soliton 'embedded' in another type, solitary waves in non-local media, quantum solitary waves, and more.

Applications of Solitons

Solitary waves of all flavours arise ubiquitously in fluid mechanics, optics, atomic physics, biophysics, and more. It is impossible to discuss these manifestations exhaustively, so we show a few exciting figures and restrict ourselves to brief discussions of some of our favourite examples:

Non-linear Optics

Solitary waves are omnipresent in non-linear optics. There have been extensive experimental and theoretical investigations about both spatial solitary waves (*Fig. 5.9*), in which non-linearity balances diffraction, and temporal solitary waves, in which nonlinearity balances dispersion. From a mathematical perspective, continuous nonlinear Schrödinger (NLS) equations are among the hallmark models in non-linear optics, as they describe dispersive envelope waves (via solitary-wave solutions of the NLS) of the electric field in optical bars, and discrete NLS (DNLS) equations can be used to describe the dynamics of pulses in, e.g., optical waveguide arrays and photorefractive crystals.

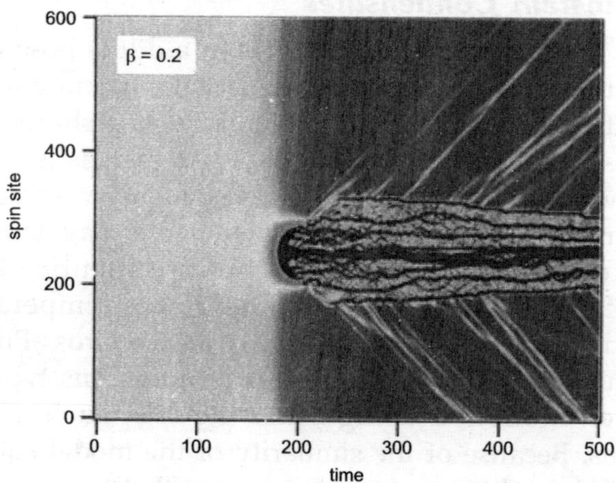

Fig. 5.9 : Simulation of spin-wave localization in an anti ferromagnet with a demagnetization field

Classes of solitary waves known as second-harmonic generation (SHG) solitary waves, which are so-named because they occur in χ^2 (second-order non-linearity) materials in optics, have been created experimentally in both spatial and temporal domains. Such materials have also been used to provide perhaps the only experimental generation of *spatiotemporal solitary waves*, in which there is a simultaneous balance of diffraction by self-focussing modulation and dispersion by phase modulation. There have also been numerous studies of *light bullets*, which are three-dimensional localized pulses in self-focussing media with anomalous group dispersion. The properties of optical solitary waves can be manipulated experimentally through both 'dispersion management' and 'nonlinearity management'. The areas with higher energy are shaded in bluer colours. The sample-shape parameter β measures the ratio of demagnetization energy to exchange energy. Initially, one observes the formation of a single broad ILM in the entire 1024-spin lattice. Energy is then rapidly transfered to a smaller region from the rest of the lattice, so that the ensuing excitation breaks up into several virtually stationary and strongly localized defects.

Bose-Einstein Condensates

At very low temperatures, particles in a dilute bose gas can occupy the same quantum (ground) state, forming a BEC, a coherent cloud of atoms which appears as a sharp peak in both position and momentum space. As the gas is cooled, a large fraction of the atoms in the gas condense via a quantum phase transition, which occurs when the wavelengths of individual atoms overlap and behave identically. The macroscopic dynamics of BECs near zero temperature is modeled by an NLS equation known as the Gross-Pitaevskii (GP) equation. BEC solitary waves of numerous types have also been modelled using other models, such as DNLS equations. Because of the similarity of the model equations, many of the solitary-wave phenomena that were originally studied in the context of non-linear optics arise here as well, and the extreme tunability of BECs has been a major boon for both theoretical and experimental studies. For example, bright solitary waves were created in ^{7}Li atoms and gap solitons have been created in ^{87}Rb Additionally, there have been several theoretical studies on manipulating the properties of solitary waves in BECs via non-linearity management (which can be achieved in principle by exploiting the properties of Feshbach resonances). Many novel types of solitary-wave structures have now been created in BEC laboratories, and research on non-linear waves in BECs continues to develop at a rapid pace. One of the most important current experimental challenges for work on solitary waves in BECs (and also non-linear optics) is the creation of stable two-dimensional and three-dimensional solitary waves in the presence of cubic self-focusing nonlinearity, as such structures (*Fig. 5.10*) must be stabilized in order to prevent them from collapsing (in accord with theoretical predictions). The intensity increases from dark to light, so these solitary waves are lower-density pulses in a higher-density background. The axial (horizontal) length of the BEC is about 250 microns.

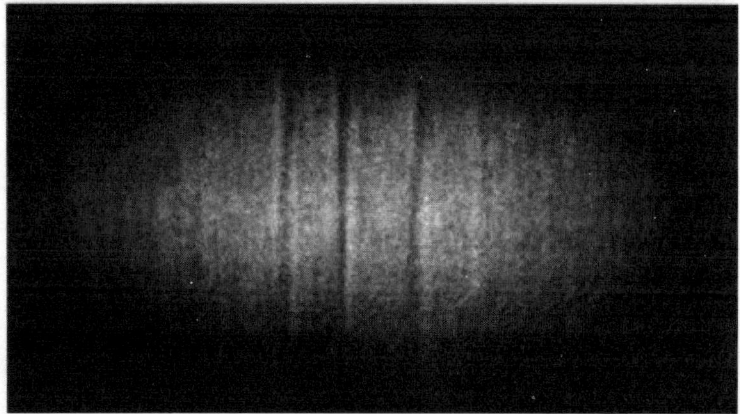

Fig. 5.10. Three dark solitary waves in an Rb Bose-Einstein condensate (BEC).

Water Waves

Russell's 'wave of translation' was a water-wave soliton, and (as discussed above) Korteweg and de Vries derived their non-linear wave equation to describe the shallow water waves that Russell had observed. The KdV equation arises in the long-wavelength limit, and shallow-water solitary waves have been the subject of numerous laboratory experiments. Solitary waves also arise in deep water (*Fig. 5.11*), as shown by the pioneering work of Vladimir Zakharov who derived an envelope wave description whose limiting case satisfies an NLS equation. Additionally, solitary-wave solutions have been constructed in more sophisticated models in fluid dynamics, and there has been a lot of work on myriad types of solitary waves. For instance, various scientists have attempted to explain the large and seemingly spontaneous *freak waves* (or *rogue waves*) as solitary waves. Additionally, *tidal bores* have been explained in terms of *dispersive shock waves*, which consist of a front followed by a train of solitary waves. Other interesting studies have focused on turbulent velocity fields that can arise from the breaking of solitary waves.

Fig. 5.11 : Recreation of Russell's Soliton in the Union Canal

Biophysics

There have been some attempts to use solitary-wave descriptions to describe various biophysical phenomena. One example is the *Davydov soliton,* which satisfies an equation that was designed to model energy transfer in hydrogen-bonded spines that stabilize protein ∝-helices. The Davydov soliton represents a state composed of an excitation of amide-I and its associated hydrogen-bond distortion. It has been used to describe a local conformational change of the DNA -helix, and there now exists experimental evidence of such states. Another type of DNA solitary wave was introduced by Peyrard and Bishop, who interpreted solitary-wave solutions of a model for DNA denaturization as bubbles that appear in the DNA structure as temperature is increased. The Peyrard-Bishop model also admits ILM solutions, and ILMs have also been investigated both theoretically and experimentally in the context of biopolymers. Using a model similar to Davydov's, local modes in molecular crystals have also been described using solitary waves. More controversially, solitary waves have recently been used in neuroscience as an alternative to the accepted Hodgkin-Huxley model to describe the travelling of signals along a cell's membrane.

Granular Crystals

Granular crystals consist of a tightly-packed array of solid particles that deform when they contact each other. They are modeled by an FPU-like set of equations with an asymmetric potential (there is only a force when the particles are squeezing each other) arising from the Hertzian description for contact between elastic particles. Granular crystals exhibit a highly non-linear dynamic response (*Fig. 5.12*), and the equations of motion give zero when they are linearized (although additional, linear forces, such as gravity and precompression, can also be included with appropriate experimental setups). Taking a long-wavelength asymptotic limit of the equations of motion gives a partial differential equation whose only diffusion term is non-linear. This equation admits travelling compacton solutions that closely match waves that have observed experimentally. Other types of

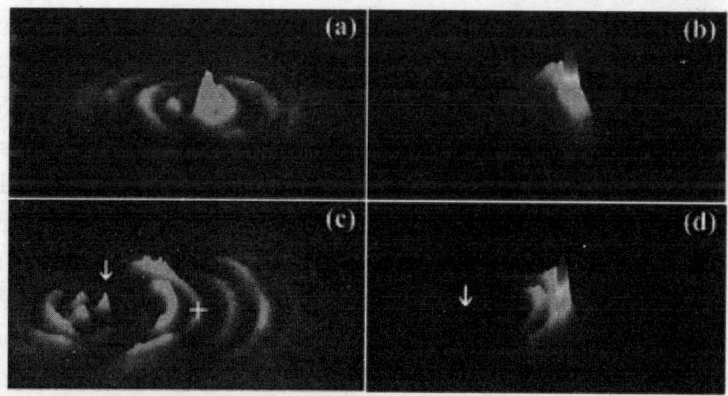

Fig. 5.12 : Transition from discrete diffraction [sub-panels (a,c)] to non-linear self-trapping [sub-panels (b, d)] of a probe beam in a ring-shaped photonic lattice.

solitary waves, including ILMs, have been observed in the presence of precompression.

Surface Waves

Numerous interesting non-linear wave phenomena can occur on the surface of a 'continuum' (e.g., fluids, solids, and appropriate granular materials which can often be modelled using continuum descriptions), and some of them admit solitary-wave descriptions. Although it can be applied more broadly, the term *surface wave* is often used to refer to a relatively specific class of examples. These include the pattern-forming standing waves called *Faraday waves* that form, e.g., on the surface of continua housed in vertically vibrated receptacles [similar phenomena have now also been seen in other settings, such as BECs soliton-like *oscillons* that switch between peaks and craters and have been demonstrated in vertically-vibrated plates of granular materials, viscous fluids, and colloids; and *acoustic surface waves*, which travel along the surfaces of solid materials.

Plasmas

One of the convenient testbeds to study the dynamics of solitary waves has been plasmas, which consist of a large number of charged particles (*Fig. 5.13*). For example, the KdV equation has been used to describe the local ion density (reflecting the local departure of the charge from neutrality) in a perturbation of the charge density. Other equations that admit soliton and solitary-wave solutions, including the Kadomtsev-Petviashvili (KP) equations and more complicated variants of both the KdV and KP equations, are also prominent in the study of plasmas. Dusty plasmas, which contain small suspended particles, have been modeled using non-linear oscillator chains that admit several types of solitary-wave solutions (such as ILMs).

Fig. 5.13 : An oscillon in a vertically-vibrated layer of bronze beads

Field Theory

Solitons and their relatives, such as instantons, are also important in both classical and quantum field theory. Topological solitons such as monopoles, kinks, vortices, and skyrmions are key to the modern understanding of field theory. (Non-topological solitons such as Q-balls have generally played a less central role than their topological counterparts.) In (1+1)-dimensional quantum field theory, topological soliton solutions of the sine-Gordon equation can be mapped to elementary excitations of the Thirring model (an exactly solvable quantum field theory). This provides a toy model for more physically relevant examples in which the role of solitons is played by magnetic monopoles that can be mapped to electrically charged elementary particles via an equivalence that is given the name *strong-weak duality* or, more commonly, *S-duality*. S-duality is also an essential feature of string theory. *Instantons* give non-perturbative corrections to path integrals, and they play a crucial role in quantum field theory (especially in tunnelling phenomena). Because of their algebraic structure, topological instantons can sometimes be constructed explicitly using methods from subjects such as twistor theory. Topological solitons also arise in various parts of string theory and supergravity (such as in studies of D-branes and NS-branes), as well as in the study of defects such as domain walls and cosmic strings.

Applications of Solitons in Biology

To understand how a soliton is instrumental in the process of catalysis, we have to understand a little of the quantum world. The common sense view, that we live in a world of 'objects' with rigidly defined boundaries, is not applicable when we begin to think about electrons, protons and the phenomena of the very small. Quantum mechanics is a statistical discipline that does not treat very small objects as exactly definable in space and time. The Uncertainty Principle portrays a world where a particle may inhabit a range of possible states. To handle this 'uncertainty,' quantum mechanics treats a particle as a wave function that encompasses its possible states. Nor is the wave function simply a convenient mathematical construct. The mathematics of probability wave functions can accurately describe the quantum world and demonstrate a high degree of consistency between the mathematics and empirical observation.

One of the surprising consequences of quantum theory is a phenomenon termed 'quantum tunnelling.' In the classical world, there are limits to what is possible. If an object does not have enough momentum to traverse a barrier, then the barrier will not be traversed. However, in the quantum world there are circumstances when this rule is broken. Imagine a barrier in the quantum world. Because of the wave description of quantum phenomena a particle cannot exist near a barrier without its wave function extending, to a degree, into the barrier itself; then, if the barrier is narrow enough, the probability-wave function may actually extend through the barrier entirely. The consequence of this is that there is a chance that the particle will 'disappear' from one side of the barrier and appear on the other side.

Just like quantum particles, molecules are also probability wave functions. The forces that may prevent a reaction from occurring spontaneously correspond to energy barriers as described above. In biologically based reactions this usually equates to the energy required to transfer an electron and/or a hydrogen nucleus (a proton) from one state (or position) to another. The bonds or forces that bind a proton or electron must first be broken, which requires energy - hence - an energy barrier. Somehow, the enzyme is able to overcome this energy barrier. Recent theoretical work suggests that the mechanism that effects this is a soliton wave.

It is thought that the enzyme 'vibrates' in a characteristic way. A characteristic of solitons is that they can travel long distances in space and/or time with very little loss of energy and structure. The effect of this is that it can transfer a coherent 'lump' of energy from one place in the enzyme to another. The effect of the soliton in the enzyme is to cause it to change shape. This change of shape causes movement among any molecules bound to the enzyme. It is theorised that the soliton causes a conformational (i.e. shape) change in the enzyme, such that the wave functions of the reagents bound to the enzyme overlap and thereby greatly increase the possibility of quantum tunnelling.

Again, as a consequence of the uncertainty principle, just as the probability wave function of a molecule means that it can occupy many potential states simultaneously, so the reagents and products of a reaction may represent simultaneous states in the overall probability description. At one level of description, therefore, we may consider the reaction as resulting from the overlapping of the wave functions of the reagents. At another level of description, the reaction occurs as a consequence of the overlapping of the potential energy surfaces of the reagents and products. Fig. 5.14, shows a simplified phase space diagram of the potential energy surfaces of the reagent(s) and product(s) of a reaction. Each point on the potential energy surface corresponds to a particular shape of the molecule (for reagent(s) and product(s)) and its associated potential energy.

In the simplified diagram, the distributions of nuclear configurations are plotted for both reactants and the products. Unusual configurations, which are less likely, have higher potential energy than more likely configurations. The two distributions, for reactants and products, may overlap as a consequence of a soliton. The transition state of the reaction occurs at the point that they intersect. The transition is thought to involve quantum tunnelling.

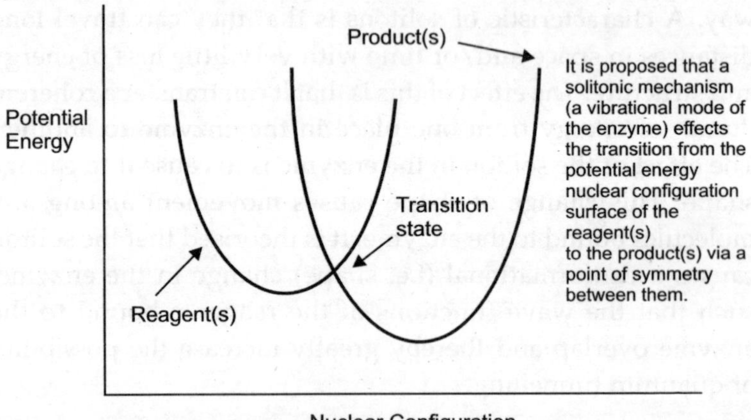

Fig. 5.14 : Quantum tunnelling

An early application of solitons in biology was proposed by Davydov (1982). He suggested that they may play a role in the process of muscle contraction and relaxation.This model also serves to introduce the concept that in living processes there exists a unique relationship between energy and structure.

The Davydov Model of Muscle Function

The basic principles of muscle contraction have been known for some time. However, the precise mechanism is still unknown or else the subject of theoretical investigation. Muscle is comprised of bundles of elongated cells called muscle fibers (*Fig. 5.15*). At the sub-cellular level, muscle fibers contain bundles of elongated structures called myofilaments. There are two types of myofilament-actin and myosin. Two sets of actin fibers are attached to membranes and face each other in a similar way that we might observe if we placed two combs together such that their teeth faced each other. Threaded between the teeth are myosin filaments—these are not attached to the membranes at either end. The entire structure of myofilaments, including the membrane at each end (termed a z-disc), is called the sarcomere. The action of muscle contraction translates, at the sub-cellular level, to a contraction of the overall length of the sarcomere. It is generally agreed that this achieved as a result of the myosin and actin myofilaments overlapping to a greater extent.

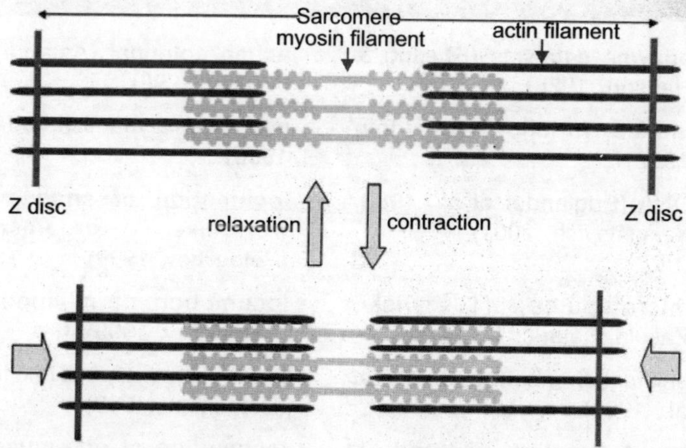

Fig. 5.15 : Davydov model of muscle function

In the Davydov model, energy released by the hydrolysis of ATP at the binding site on the myosin molecule is translated into kinetic energy. Normally, this energy would be expected to quickly dissipate. However, Davydov noted that the structure of myosin was comprised of regularly spaced pairs of oxygen and carbon atoms that would give rise to a compressive force that would cancel out the dissipative tendency of the energy wave. Consequently, a highly concentrated 'lump' of energy in the form of a soliton wave would progress as a deformation of the myosin filament. This deformation would provide sufficient localized kinetic energy such that the myosin heads that protrude from the @-helix protein strands at their ends would slide and interlock (or 'ratchet') with the surrounding actin filaments causing the overall length of the sarcomere to decrease.

In addition to the above examples there are many other biological processes in which solitons have been suggested as mechanisms of function.

Biological Processes where solitons have been theorized

Microscopic Solitons in biology	Macroscopic Solitons in biology
• enzyme catalysis (Ebeling & Hanson, 1988)	• action potential (Aslandi & Mornev, 1996)
• muscle function (Davydov, 1982)?	• population dynamics (Odell, 1980)
• DNA (Englander et al., 1980; Yakushevich, 2001)	• locomotion of snail and worm-like organisms (Petoukhov, 1999)
• microtubules (Tuszynski, Zakula, Sataric, 1992)	• locomotion of millipedes (Petoukhov, 1999)
• cell membranes (eg, Sataric et al., 1991)	• locomotion of snakes and fish (Petoukhov, 1999)
• heart function (Aslandi & Mornev, 1999)	• locomotion of non-muscle motor systems (Petoukhov, 1999)
• protein folding (Caspi & Ben-Jacob, 2001)	• conformations of biological bodies (Petoukhov, 1999)

Scale Invariance in Biology

The possibility of scale invariant processes in biology is supported by the work of Brown, Enquist and West (1997, 1999). They have investigated scaling laws in biological structures and processes (*Fig. 5.16*). Below we see a continuous relationship between the log of the body mass and the log of the rate of metabolism from the scale of the enzyme to the elephant.

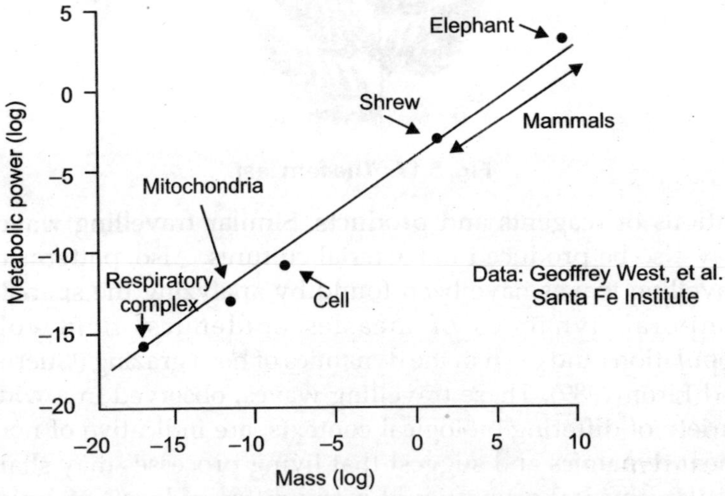

Fig. 5.16 : Universal scaling

In addition to the metabolic rate/mass law illustrated above, they have found simple universal scaling laws that can be used to predict the structural and functional properties of vertebrate cardiovascular and respiratory systems, plant vascular systems, and insect tracheal tubes. Below is a commonly cited example of a fractal in biology—the fern leaf: (*Fig. 5.17*)

In addition to the above examples more subtle instances of scale invariance in biology may be cited. Oscillating catalyzed reactions may give rise to characteristic travelling waves (generally agreed to be solitons) of different concen-

Fig. 5.17 : The fern leaf

trations of reagents and products. Similar travelling waves may also be produced in bacterial cultures. Also, patterns of travelling waves have been found by analyzing the spatial/temporal dynamics of measles epidemics, field vole populations and even in the dynamics of herd grazing (Gueron and Liron 1989). These travelling waves, observed in a wide variety of differing biological contexts, are indicative of non-linear dynamics and suggest that living processes may share similar physical properties at many different levels of scale.

BZ reaction
Travelling waves formed by oscillating catlyzed reactions
Pictures taken by P. Ruoff, Stavanger College, Norway
Reproduced with his kind permission

Fig. 5.18 : Invariant catalytic mod

More direct support of the scale invariant catalytic model may be found by comparing two ostensibly different biological processes—protein folding and muscle function. A solitonic mechanism has been proposed as the principle agent in the process of protein folding and conformational changes. On the surface, this process does not appear to be catalytic in nature - there is no enzyme involved. However, it has already been argued that the principle agent of catalysis is not the enzyme per se, but a vibrational mode of the enzyme—the soliton (*Fig. 5.18*).

Let us consider what happens in the case of a catalysed chemical reaction. Before the catalyst is added and the reaction has not yet occurred the solution is out of equilibrium. However, it is clear that the solution is stable. This may be described as a meta-stable state. The action of the catalyst is to effect a transition from a meta-stable state to the ground state via a chemical reaction. Likewise, in the case of an unfolded protein, in as far as the protein is stable it is described as being in a meta-stable state. Again, the action of the soliton is to effect a transition from a meta-stable state to the ground state via, in this case, a conformational change. What is suggested here is that the soliton may be described as catalytic in that it effects transitions to more favourable thermodynamic states. Whether this is achieved as a result of a chemical reaction or a conformational change is simply a matter of contingency. Given that the soliton is the principle agent of catalysis let us re-examine the Davydov model of muscle function in the light of this (*Fig. 5.19*) no chemical

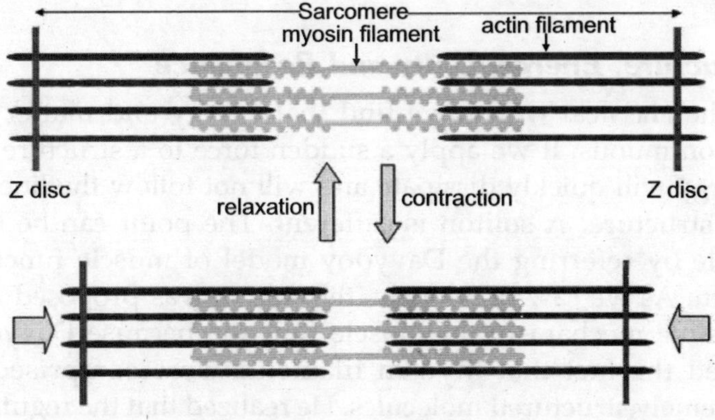

Fig. 5.19 : Vibrational mode of the enzyme—the soliton

reaction or conformational change in the body defies the laws of thermodynamics. From this it follows that whatever changes take place in the body they are always to thermodynamically favourable states. The fact that muscles can both relax and contract would seem to imply that this is not the case. However, we must remember that the most favourable state (or ground state) is dependent upon local thermodynamic conditions. Changes in the local chemical and structural environment of actin and myosin molecules within the cell may alter the local thermodynamics such that what was previously the ground state configuration may suddenly become a met-stable state (with no alteration of configuration) and thus be out of equilibrium. If the soliton is the principle agent of muscle function, then the action of the Davydov soliton, whether during relaxation or contraction, is to effect a transition from a meta-stable configuration of actin relative to myosin to the ground state configuration. It should be pointed out that the Davydov model of muscle function is not widely accepted. However, the broad thrust of this argument does not depend on the Davydov model alone. Increasingly, solitons are being implicated in a wide range of biological processes which in itself represents evidence of the importance of the soliton in biology and points to the possibility of a scale invariant catalytic theme.

Structure, Energy, Unity and Resonance

In the classical world, we find that energy and matter are discontinuous. If we apply a sudden force to a structure the energy will quickly dissipate and will not follow the lines of the structure. A soliton is different. The point can be best made by referring the Davydov model of muscle function again. As we saw previously, the soliton was proposed as a possible mechanism for muscle function because Davydov noted the fact that Myosin filaments were comprised of extremely structured molecules. He realized that the regularly spaced molecules could support a soliton. The important point here is that for the soliton to exist at all there must be structure in the boundary conditions - in this case, this corresponds to the regularly spaced carbon and oxygen atoms. The regularly spaced carbon and oxygen atoms constitute a symmetry or invariance. The soliton, therefore, dynamically involves the symmetry or invariance 'implicit' in the structure such that energy and structure become continuous—they work together. Consequently, the 'implicit' structure (invariance) of the actin molecule is made 'explicit' as a unified non-linear dynamic—a soliton wave.

It is suggested that a major effect of a soliton is to unite structures by 'utilizing the invariance that they embody. Earlier, a potential problem concerning the relationship between function and persistence was addressed by demonstrating the possibility that 'apparent function' and metabolism (as a process of catalysis) were identical. A similar problem arises when we consider that biological processes require energy. Energy almost invariably imposes stresses upon structures. However, if energy in biological processes utilizes the symmetry (invariance) implicit in biological structures via a solitonic mechanism, then there is a continuous relationship between energy and structure.

Although solitons are not strictly speaking resonant phenomena, there are, nevertheless, similarities. Solitons can only exist if there is a high degree of invariance (structure or pattern) in the medium and/or boundary conditions. Also, a particular medium and set of boundary conditions will only support a soliton of a particular structure and energy. If solitons are indeed a principle biological mechanism then they are 'utilizing' the symmetries of the environment such that energy and structure come together.

Important Applications of Soliton

Solitons in Standard Telecom Fiber

As a quantitative example, solitons in standard telecom fibers single-mode fibers for the 1.5-μm spectral region) can be considered. Assuming the common SMF-28e fiber of Corning, the effective mode area is 85 μm^2 at 1550 nm wavelength, resulting in a non-linear coefficient of 1.43 mrad/(W – m). The chromatic dispersion at 1550 nm is +16.2 ps/(nm – km), corresponding to "20 660 fs^2/m. Using the above equation, we find that 1-ps solitons have to have a pulse energy of 51 pJ, corresponding to a peak power of 45 W. For 10 times shorter solitons with a 100-fs duration, the pulse energy rises 10-fold to 510 pJ, whereas the peak power becomes 100 times larger (4.5 kW).

Soliton Self-Frequency Shift

When propagating in an optical fiber, soliton pulses are subject not only to the Kerr non-linearity, but also to stimulated Raman scattering. For very short solitons (with durations of e.g. <100 fs), the optical spectrum becomes so broad that the longer-wavelength tail can experience Raman amplification at the expense of power in the shorter-wavelength tail. This causes an overall spectral shift of the soliton towards longer wavelengths, i.e., a *soliton self-frequency shift*. The strength of this effect depends strongly on the pulse duration, since shorter solitons exhibit a higher peak power and a broader optical spectrum. The latter is important because the Raman gain is weak for small frequency offsets. During propagation, the rate of the frequency shift often slows down, because the pulse energy is reduced and the pulse duration increased[24].

The soliton self-frequency shift can be exploited for reaching spectral regions which are otherwise difficult to access. By adjusting the pulse energy in the fiber, it is possible to tune the output wavelength in a large range[25].

The Contribution of Optical Fiber

This invention relates generally to broadband communications systems, such as cable television systems and the optical equipment used in such systems, and more specifically to the transmission of optical signals in a broadband communication system.

Communication systems, such as a cable television system, include a headend section for receiving satellite signals and demodulating the signals to baseband. The baseband signal is then converted to an optical signal for transmission from the headend section over fiber optic cable. Optical transmitters are utilized within the cable system for imprinting radio frequency (RF) signal information onto an optical beam, where the optical signal is then split and applied to various optical fibers within the transmitter for transmission to remotely located optical receivers. The optical receivers are provided for receiving the optical signals and converting the optical signals back to RF signals, which are further transmitted along branches of the system over coaxial cable rather than fiber optic cable. Taps are situated along the coaxial cable to tap off a portion of the signal to subscribers of the system.

A primary aim of communication systems is to provide the highest quality signal to each subscriber on the network. It is, therefore, important to understand the parameters that affect network planning and implementation. Prominent among these parameters are amplitudes of the optical signal carriers, i.e., carrier level, and noise. It is well known that noise exists in conventional electrical systems, as well as optical systems, in which noise is further classified as thermal, shot, and relative intensity noise (RIN), the latter being exclusive to optical transmission systems. Carrier-to-noise ratio (CNR) is a useful measurement of the effects of noise upon signals. A goal of most high quality services delivery networks is to maintain the ratio of carrier signal level to noise as high as possible. The maintenance of a high CNR becomes more important as networks grow larger and implement two-way services.

Although employing simplistic techniques, such as decreasing the fiber lengths between optical nodes, can mitigate CNR problems, such techniques decrease the number of users served by the network, decrease the network's physical reach, decrease the value of the network to its users, and ultimately, increase costs to both subscribers and service providers. Thus, any solution to the problem of degradation of CNR in large system networks should offer a better way to provide reliable and accurate transmission of optical signals within a cable television system while maintaining or increasing all existing functionality.

The method and apparatus within an optical transmitter for suppressing relative intensity noise (RIN) by generating at least two optical signals, each having differing wavelengths and combining the optical signals with a combiner into a composite output signal, wherein the composite output signal has an output power value equal to the sum of the power value of the optical signals. The composite output signal is then transmitted over a communication medium, wherein information content of the optical signals are substantially equivalent, and wherein combining the optical signals before transmitting provides a reduction in RIN of the composite output signal compared to the RIN of a single optical signal transmitted over a communication medium.

1. A method in a transmitter for suppressing relative intensity noise (RIN), the method comprising the steps of: generating a first signal having a power value and a first wavelength; generating a second signal having a power value and a second wavelength; adjusting the power value of the first signal and the power value of the second signal; combining the first and second signals into a single output signal, wherein the single output signal has an output power value equal to the sum of the adjusted power value of the first signal and the adjusted power value of the second signal; and transmitting the single output signal over a communication medium, wherein information content of the first and second signals is substantially equivalent; and wherein combining the first and second signals before transmitting provides a reduction in RIN of the single output signal.

2. An optical transmitter for transmitting signals that include information, the optical transmitter comprising: at least two optical sources for generating optical signals each having a substantially equal power value and each having a different wavelength; a phase delay element coupled to an output port of at least one of the optical sources, wherein the phase delay element delays at least one of the optical signals a combiner for combining the optical signals into a composite signal, wherein the composite signal has an output power value equal to the sum of the power values associated with the optical signals; and an output coupled to the combiner for transmitting the composite signal, wherein transmission of the composite signal provides a reduction in relative intensity noise.
3. A communications system for transmitting information, the communications system comprising: an optical transmitter, comprising: at least two optical sources for generating optical signals each having a substantially equal power value and each having a different wavelength; a phase delay element coupled to an output port of at least one of the optical sources, wherein the phase delay element delays at least one of the optical signals; a combiner for combining the optical signals into a composite signal, wherein the composite signal has an output power value equal to the sum of the power values associated with the optical signals; a modulator for modulating the composite signal; and an output port coupled to the modulator for transmitting the composite signal along a transmission medium; and an optical receiver coupled to the optical transmitter for receiving the composite signal, wherein the composite signal provides a reduction in relative intensity noise of at least 3 dB.
4. A method of measuring relative intensity noise (RIN), the method comprising the steps of: generating at least two optical signals, each having a substantially equal

power value and each having a different wavelength; combining the optical signals into a composite signal, wherein the composite signal has an output power value equal to the sum of the power values associated with the optical signals; and measuring a level of the composite signal, such measurement associated with a value of RIN, and wherein the value of RIN is indicative of a reduction substantially equal to ten times logarithm of the number of optical signals.

5. A method in an optical transmitter for suppressing relative intensity noise (RIN), the method comprising the steps of: receiving an input RF signal; splitting the input RF signal into at least two RF signals having substantially equal information content; generating at least two optical signals each having a power value and differing wavelengths, the at least two optical signals each associated with one of the at least two RF signals; and combining the at least two optical signals into a composite signal, wherein the composite signal has an output power value equal to the sum of the power value of the at least two optical signals, wherein the composite signal provides a reduction in RIN as compared to the RIN if a single one of the optical signals, at a greater power, such as two times the power if two optical signals are provided, had been transmitted by itself.

6. A communications system for transmitting information, the communications system comprising: an optical transmitter, comprising: at least two optical sources for generating optical signals each having a substantially equal power value and each having a different wavelength; a combiner for combining the optical signals into a composite signal, wherein the composite signal has an output power value equal to the sum of the power values associated with the optical signals; a modulator for modulating the composite signal; and an output port coupled to the modulator

for transmitting the composite signal along a transmission medium; and a splitter for splitting the composite signal into a first and second signal; and two receivers coupled to the splitter each for receiving respectively the first and second signal of the composite signal, wherein the first and second signal each provides a reduction in relative intensity noise of at least 3 dB. The communications system further comprising an amplifier coupled to one output of the splitter for amplifying the second signal.

7. Impressive progress has recently been made in the field of optical telecommunications. Systems are now being installed that permit transmission of data at a rate of many megabits/sec over distances of several kilometers between repeaters. However, since the economics of systems, such as, for instance, intercontinental submarine cable systems, are strongly affected by data rate and repeater spacing, work directed towards improvement in such system parameters continues.
8. High data rate fiber telecommunication systems typically are, and will likely continue to be, digital systems, and this application is concerned only with digital systems. Furthermore, this application is concerned only with digital fiber telecommunication systems using monomode fiber.
9. Although currently available fiber can transmit signals with relatively low loss and low dispersion, and although further improvement in these parameters can reasonably be anticipated, fiber telecommunication links require, and likely will continue to require, regeneration of the signal at so-called 'repeaters' at points intermediate between the sending or input end and the receiving or output end of the fiber communication channel. 'Input end' and 'output end' refer, of course, to a single transmission, and can be reversed for a subsequent transmission.

10. Repeaters typically carry out two functions, namely, raising the power level of the signal pulse, and reshaping the pulse. In addition, repeaters frequently also retime the pulse. Raising of the power level is required due to the attenuation suffered by the signal in any real fiber. Reshaping is required because, due to dispersive effects of the fiber, pulses typically spread. And retiming is found to be often necessary to maintain proper pulse spacing.
11. Repeaters in fiber telecommunication systems typically comprise means for detecting the signal, e.g., a photodiode, means for operating on the output of the photo detector, e.g., amplifying and reshaping the electrical output signal of the detector, and a source for optical radiation, modulated typically by the amplified and reshaped output signal of the detector, as well as means for again coupling the output of the optical source into the fiber. Repeaters of the type described are not only being used now but are being considered also for future fiber telecommunication systems[26].
12. Conventional repeaters are typically complex devices containing a significant number of components. For instance, a typical optical regenerator contains around 50 transistors. This 'electronic' complexity, particularly in high bit-rate systems, as well as reliability problems encountered with laser sources, is making repeater costs a major cost item for the fiber telecommunication systems that are currently under consideration.
13. The conventional response to these facts has, inter alia, been an effort to improve fiber quality, with the results that now repeater spacing of about 50-km appear feasible. Nevertheless, difficulties associated with the use of repeaters are sufficiently severe to make consideration of alternative solutions important,

and this application pertains to such an alternative solution. We will next discuss some fiber characteristics relevant to the invention.

14. Pulses of electromagnetic energy transmitted through optical fiber experience attenuation and dispersion, with the latter resulting in a broadening of the pulse in the time domain. If such broadening is sufficiently severe, adjacent pulses can overlap, resulting in loss of signal detectability. In monomode fiber, (i.e., fiber in which only the fundamental mode of the signal can propagate at the operating wavelength of the system) the two principal dispersion mechanisms are material dispersion and waveguide dispersion. A material of index of refraction n exhibits material dispersion at the wavelength λ if $d^2 n/d\lambda^2 \neq 0$ at that wavelength. Physically, this implies that the phase velocity of a plane wave travelling in such a medium varies non-linearly with wavelength, and consequently a light pulse will broaden as it travels through such medium. Waveguide dispersion typically also is wavelength dependent. We will refer herein to the combined material and waveguide dispersion as 'chromatic' dispersion. As an example, typical of magnitudes of chromatic dispersion effects in a typical monomode fiber, a 10 ps pulse of carrier wavelength 1.5 ìm doubles its width after about 650 meters.

15. If in a medium $d^2n/d\lambda^2 > 0$ throughout a certain wavelength regime, then the medium is said to be normally dispersive in that regime. On the other hand, a wavelength regime throughout which $d^2n/d\lambda^2 < 0$ constitutes a so-called anomalous dispersion regime. In silica, for instance, a regime of normal dispersion extends from short wavelengths to about 1.27 μm, and an anomalous dispersion regime from about 1.27 μm to longer wavelengths. Separating the two regimes is a wavelength at which $d^2n/d\lambda^2 = 0$ i.e., at which material dispersion is zero to first order. This

wavelength depends on the composition of the medium. The wavelength at which chromatic dispersion vanishes to first order similarly is composition dependent and, in addition, depends on such fiber parameters as diameter and doping profile. It can, for instance, be as high as about 1.5 μm in appropriately designed monomode silica-based fibers.

16. A natural choice of carrier wavelength in a high data rate fiber telecommunication system is the wavelength of first-order zero chromatic dispersion in the fiber. However, even at this wavelength, pulse spreading occurs due to higher order terms in the dispersion[27].
17. Recently, it has been proposed to use the nonlinear change of dielectric constant (Kerr effect) of a monomode fiber to compensate for the effect of chromatic dispersion, i.e., to utilize 'solitons.' For purposes of this application, we mean by 'soliton' a pulse of electromagnetic radiation that propagates in monomode optical fiber with a characteristic constant shape.
18. A soliton pulse occurs when the broadening effect due to chromatic dispersion is balanced by a contraction due to the non-linear dependence of the index of refraction on electric field. The existence of solitons in monomode fiber and the possibility of their stationary transmission was predicted with lossless monomode fibers, and taught the existence of a minimum pulse peak power, dependent, inter alia, on fiber parameters, pulse width and carrier wavelength, above which solitons can exist. These predictions of Hasegawa and Tappert[28] have been verified, for instance, by demonstrating dispersionless transmission of a 7 ps pulse with a peak power of about 1 Watt at 1.45 μm through monomode fiber for a distance of about 700 meters. Mollenauer et. al.[29] also verified the prediction by Hasegawa and Tappert that

soliton pulses of peak power in excess of the so-called 'balanced' peak power P_o undergo pulse narrowing.

19. The conclusion drawn from the optical fiber is that a method and a system for transmitting a pulse of electromagnetic radiation, of carrier wavelength λ_o, through a fiber communication channel. The channel comprises single mode optical fiber, with λ_o being a wavelength in the anomalous dispersion regime of the fiber. The method comprises coupling the pulse into the input end of the fiber, such that a soliton pulse, preferably a single soliton, is formed and propagates. The method further comprises amplifying the soliton pulse by non-electronic amplifying means located intermediate the input end and the output end of the channel, preferably without re-shaping the pulse, except as the pulse shape changes due to the soliton nature of the pulse. The disclosed system for transmitting the pulse comprises means for coupling the pulse into the fiber, and means for non-electronically amplifying the pulse, the latter means being located intermediate the input end and the output end of the channel.
20. It is comtemplated that the invention can be practiced by employing any appropriate non-electronic amplifying means. Exemplary means are a glass amplifier, i.e., a glass medium, typically a fiber, doped with an appropriate ion species (that is, ions having energy levels separated by an energy substantially equal to hc/λ_o, where h is Planck's constant and c is the speed of light in vacuum), ad pumped with electromagnetic radiation adapted to producing a population inversion in the energy levels. Another exemplary amplifying means is a Raman amplifier, e.g., a glass medium, typically a fiber, in which λ_o is within a 'Stokes' wavelength band of a pump radiation[30]. Still another exemplary amplifying means is injection of a

continuous wave (cw) of wavelength essentially equal to λ_o, in phase with the soliton, and of amplitude substantially lower than the pulse amplitude, whereby, through nonlinear interaction between pulse and cw, a pulse amplitude increase can result. And still another exemplary amplifying means is a semiconductor laser operated as an amplifying medium.

The above exemplary means are examples of "non-electronic" amplifying means, i.e., means in which the signal is at all times present in the form of a photon pulse, and is never present as an electron pulse. Amplifying means useful in the practice of the invention are non-electronic amplifying means, since they permit preservation of the phase of the pulse.

It will be appreciated that a soliton pulse does not attain its final (i.e., asymptotic) shape and pulse height at the moment of 'amplification,' i.e., when energy is transferred to the pulse, but rather, the pulse typically undergoes a change of pulse width and amplitude while 'amplification,' to attain its final shape and amplitude after propagation for a distance of the order of L_{NL}, to be defined below. We herein contemplate amplification in this extended sense.

It is advantageous to choose the initial pulse power and pulse width as well as the amplifier spacing and amplification factors such that the above-referred-to changes are a pulse narrowing and an amplitude increase.

Nematic Liquid Crystals and Optical Solitons

This invention concerns with optical fiber soliton telecommunication systems. The propagation speed of optical solitons in single mode optical fiber depends on the wavelength of the solitons. Thus, if solitons of different wavelengths are copropagating, 'collisions' between pulses can be expected to result. Collisions between solitons do preserve the soliton character of the colliding pulses, even in the presence of perturbations of the type present in fiber communications systems, e.g., core size variations, distributed or lumped loss, and distributed gain; thus, a wavelength division multiplexed soliton system is possible, and techniques and formulae for the design of such systems are disclosed. In preferred embodiments, fiber loss is periodically compensated by Raman gain. Typical amplification periods (using currently available silica-based fiber) are 30-50-km, typical pump powers are less than 100 mW, and rate-length products of the order of 3 105 GHz-km are possible. Multiplexed soliton systems have several advantages over prior art soliton systems. For instance, they permit attainment of very high transmission rates without the use of very high speed electronics. For instance, an examplary 3000-km, 24 channel multiplexed soliton system has a total transmission rate of 106 GHz, i.e., 4.5 GHz/channel.

In modern telecommunications the development of all-optical equivalents for electronic signal processing devices has been the topic of much on-going research and development effort. This research area is focussed on the development of optical signal switching using liquid crystals. This figure shows two nematicons interacting. They are out of phase and form a dipole.

Two-dimensional, spatial, optical solitary waves, termed nematicons, can form in liquid crystals due to a balance of the non-local response of the nematic with the diffractive spreading of the light. Liquid crystals have the potential for the development of compact photonic devices and could be the basis of optical switches in devices which do not need to operate at the large GHz telecommunication repetition rates. An advantage of photonic devices based on liquid crystals is that a nematicon can form a waveguide through which another nematicon can propagate, thus forming a light 'circuit' which is easily re-configurable. It is anticipated that these re-configurable light circuits could form the basis for a wide variety of photonic devices.

Simulation of Soliton Propagation

Soliton propagation, possibly with additional disturbing effects, can be investigated with numerical simulations . There are also some analytical tools, e.g. *soliton perturbation theory*, involving dynamic equations for small deviations of pulse parameters from those of the ideal soliton.

Spatial Solitons

Apart from the temporal solitons as discussed above, there are also *spatial solitons*. In that case, a non-linearity of the medium cancels the diffraction, so that a beam with constant beam radius can be formed even in a medium which would be homogeneous without the influence of the light beam.

Even more exotic are quadratic solitons supported by second-order nonlinearities. In this case the main physics comes from the phase-matched parametric interaction between different frequency components of the optical field. All three types of spatial optical solitons can be generated by a coherent source, and they present a classical example of self-localization via coherent interaction. Nevertheless, shortly after the discovery of photorefractive solitons, it was shown that beam coherence was not necessary for soliton formation, an unexpected and surprising result at that time. This research ultimately led to the discovery of 'white light' solitons, in which the light is both spatial and temporally incoherent. The incoherent soliton, discovered by Segev, Christodoulides *et al.*, provides a counter-intuitive generalization of the concept of light self-trapping and spatial solitons. A classical spatial soliton is generated by a continuous source, specifically a cw beam.However, self-trapping may also occur for a pulse propagating in a bulk medium. Such a pulse—self-trapped in both space and time—is called an 'optical bullet,' and in communications it can be used as an information carrier since it is an elementary bit that does not spread in the presence of either dispersion or diffraction. Up to now, light bullets have not been generated in an experiment, although a close approximation has been observed, by use of "cascading" quadratic nonlinearity, a two-dimensional beam self-trapped in time and one spatial dimension was demonstrated by Wise and co-workers[31]. Today, many different types of spatial optical solitons and many different realizations of the soliton concept are known. Spatial solitons can be excited in waveguide arrays, they can appear in resonators and optical cavities as cavity solitons, they can be supported by mixed interaction as magneto-optic solitons, and so forth. In defocusing optical media, spatial solitons appear as dark solitons and optical vortices[32].

Soliton-induced Waveguides and Circuits

Because a spatial optical soliton changes the refractive index of the optical medium where it propagates and can attract and guide beams, the soliton can be considered as inducing optical waveguides that can guide another beam of a different wavelength or polarization, through the effect of induced cross-phase modulation[33]. Many such 'colliding waveguides' may create a self-reconfigurable waveguide circuit which forms a virtual circuitry[34] and offers potential advantages over more conventional waveguides and devices. This kind of integrated optical circuit relies on the basic property of soliton beams: they can pass through one another without significantly influencing each other. One can write soliton-induced waveguide circuits in photosensitive materials in which one light-written structure can be erased and replaced by another. These useful properties of spatial solitons open the door for the design of dense, reconfigurable self-induced optical waveguide interconnects.

Soliton Flowers: Necklaces, Multipoles, and Propellers

Solitons behave like real particles and exhibit 'forces' during interactions. The de-Broglie wave representation of real particles shares many properties with selftrapped wave packets and solitons. Research into this analogy recently led to the concept of 'light molecules',[35].

Multicomponent spatial solitons which can be regarded as more complex composite objects consisting of coupled states of simpler, scalar solitons (or 'atoms'). This concept has been confirmed experimentally by realization of so-called dipole-mode vector solitons[36]. To understand why such multimode solitons can exist, one needs to keep in mind the fact that a radially symmetric optical waveguide can support a variety of transverse guided modes which correspond to dipole, quadrupole, and higherpossible for the first time, including graphic demonstrations of concepts such as soliton robustness and interactions. In the field of optics, the first observation of what we now refer to as a soliton involved spatial solitons and was made by Bjorkholm and Ashkin in the early 1970s. The researchers observed a beam whose spatial dimensions did not spread in space in either transverse dimension. Unfortunately, this pioneering experiment was 'before its time' and did not immediately stimulate further work. The study of spatial optical solitons in the 'golden age' of the 1990s led to a revolution in our thinking about optical solitons and, generally speaking, about solitary waves in realistic physical systems not described by the familiar non-linear Schrödinger equation. It was found that, contrary to the case of glass fibers, solitons are not limited to media with Kerr non-linearities. Obviously, many of the new spatial solitons discovered recently are directly related to the material properties and the variety of physical mechanisms which lead to self-trapping. One can define three major classes of spatial optical solitons based on the physics of non-linearity employed:

- Kerr and Kerr-like solitons;
- photorefractive solitons; and
- quadratic or parametric solitons.

For example, all Kerr and Kerr-like solitons rely primarily on any physical effect which produces an intensity-dependent change in refractive index. The origin can be electronic, thermal, a result of carrier.

Diffraction Management

The three main types of spatial solitons discussed above are all associated with a different type of non-linear response of an optical medium. However, since a soliton appears as a result of balance between non-linearity and diffraction, we may modify the soliton properties by changing the effective diffraction. This is the case of localized structures created in Bragg gratings and photonic crystals. Photonic crystals, an analog of semiconductors for light waves, are composite materials with periodic properties in which the propagation of photons with certain wavelengths is forbidden. They appeared first as a theoretical proposal about 10 years ago, but rapid progress in manufacturing such new engineered materials at microwave and then optical wavelengths has involved the development of new fundamental physical concepts and ideas[37]. These artificial crystalline structures provide novel and unique ways of controlling many aspects of electromagnetic radiation, and the study of the non-linear properties of such materials opens a door for realizing the concept of light-induced radiation control. Photonic crystals composed of a material with a non-linear Kerr-type response, or photonic crystals with embedded non-linear impurities, create an ideal environment for the generation and observation A simple example of the structure in which non-linear localized modes can be created is a 2D lattice of rods of smaller radius possessing a nonlinear Kerr response. Such a non-linear photonic crystal, in which the mode can be localized due to non-linearity in all directions, corresponds to a 2D spatial soliton. Spatial solitons in 2D photonic crystals have been found numerically[38] for the case in which the linear rods are made from GaAs, whereas the non-linear rods are made from a non-linear Kerr material. At first glance, this mode can be regarded as a donor state created by a single defect rod with larger dielectric constant, but in fact it exists in a perfect crystal solely due to its non-linear properties. According to more detailed studies based on effective discrete equations, the periodic environment creates an effectively longrange interaction between the field localized on the non-linear rods in the photonic crystals, allowing efficient diffraction management and stabilization of the non-linear modes, even in a Kerr medium at low powers,which is known to exhibit collapse in homogeneous media. Discrete spatial solitons and diffraction management were studied theoretically and observed experimentally for 1D arrays of optical waveguides[39]. The stable self-trapping effect predicted for 2D photonic crystals with Kerr non-linearity gives us another example of the unique properties of photonic crystals in which one can manipulate with diffraction instead of non-linearity.

Impact on Other Fields

Rapid progress in the area of spatial solitons has occurred in connection with the study of localized coherent structures in other fields. The most impressive progress has been made in the study of non-linear matter waves and Bose-Einstein condensates (BEC), where localized structures in the form of dark solitons and vortices can be generated and studied experimentally. BEC, a state of matter in which a macroscopic number of particles share the same quantum state, constitutes a well-researched example of a superfluid in which topological defects with a circulating persistent current are observed. Nearly 75 years ago, Bose and Einstein introduced the idea of a condensate of a dilute gas at temperatures close to absolute zero. BEC was experimentally created in 1995 by the JILA group[40] which trapped thousands (later, millions) of alkali 87Rb atoms in acloud and then cooled them to a millionth of a degree above absolute zero. The study of vortices and dark solitons in BEC promises to lead to a deeper understanding of a possible link between the physics of superfluidity, condensation, and non-linear optics. Extensive studies of spatial solitons in non-linear optics, in particular, of dark solitons and optical vortices, provides guidance for the further exploration of nonlinear matter waves. In particular, the transverse dynamical instability of soliton stripes in a bulk medium and the scenario of soliton decay into vortex-antivortex pairs first studied in optics is similar to that observed recently at JILA for BEC. Many ideas regarding phase imprinting now used in the BEC experiments are driven by earlier experiments on singular optical beams and vortex solitons. Moreover, the concept of BEC collapse and self explosion developed recently at JILA[41] is a direct manifestation of extensive knowledge accumulated in the study of beam self-trapping and self-focussing in non-linear optics.

A Valuable Technology for the Future

There are a number of properties of solitons which make them promising for future applications in optics. For example, the temporal signal waveforms supported by dispersion management for long-haul communications in fibers and repeated periodically are a close cousin to solitons. There are also potential applications of spatial solitons. For example, the 'perfect' beam profile associated with a soliton could be used to produce clean beams in parametric devices such as an optical parametric generator (OPG) and optical parametric amplifier (OPA). Somewhat more futuristic is the use of solitons as reconfigurable waveguides. Here, the soliton-induced waveguide can be used to trap signal beams and redirect them (and the soliton) with electrically induced deflectors to an array of output channels. The advantage of this approach is the non-diffracting nature of the solitons, and hence a high packing density for all-optical interconnects. Other applications center on some of the unique properties of soliton collisions. They can be used for implementing logic functions, or even computation, thanks again to the high packing density achievable with soliton beams. A special case is the transfer of energy between the different components of a composite soliton on collision. It is concluded in this spacial Soliton is that Solitons are truly unique entities. One of their most fascinating features is that whether the wave motion is acoustic, optical, or electrical, all solitons exhibit universal properties which transcend detailed physical mechanisms and generating equations. They exist by virtue of very strong nonlinear coupling between radiation and matter.

Spatial Optical Solitons and Soliton Clusters carrying an Angular Momentum

We describe different types of ring-profile optical solitary wave and clusters of fundamental solitons propagating in isotropic non-linear optical media. Such ringlike solitons carry a finite angular momentum and, depending on the value of the total momentum and structure, they either fragment quickly into several fundamental solitons that fly off the ring, or propagate stably for many diffraction lengths with rotating intensity and phase. Stabilization of the ring-profile optical beams and rotating soliton clusters due to vectorial interaction is also demonstrated.

Recent progress in generating spatial optical solitons in non-linear bulk media opens the possibility to study truly two dimensional self-trapping of light and interaction of multidimensional solitary waves[42]. Since the pioneering paper by Chiao *et al*[43], optical self-trapped beams are usually associated with the structure of the *fundamental* guided modes (i.e. modes without nodes). However, it has also been known for many years that light self-trapping may also occur for higher-order beams of a radial symmetry (beams with surrounding rings)[44]. More recently, self-trapped azimuthally periodically modulated beams, 'necklace beams', were shown to exist exhibiting quasi-stable expansion even in a self-focusing Kerr medium[45]. All such self-trapped optical structures possess *zero angular momentum*, and thus they do not exhibit rotation during propagation, and they are either unstable or slowly expanding beams. A novel class of optical self-trapped beams associated with the rotation of the field phase was introduced by Kruglov and Vlasov[46]. The intensity of such a beam vanishes at the beam centre, and, at the same time, the beam remains localized propagating in the form of a ringlike beam. The beam phase has a spiral structure with a singularity at the origin, representing *a phase dislocation* of the wavefront and resembling the structure of an optical vortex[47]. Therefore, such a beam can be associated with a *spatial optical soliton* of a higher order that carries a *nonzero angular momentum,* or *vortex soliton.* Subsequently, similar ringlike vortex solitons were re-discovered in other studies[48-50] and for other types of nonlinear optical medium, including quadratic non-linear media[51 52]. Furthermore, it was demonstrated in many numerical and analytical studies that such ring-profile vortex beams undergo an azimuthal symmetry-breaking instability, and they usually decay into $2|m|$ for the Kerr-like medium[48,49,51] or $2|m| + 1$ (for the quadratic media[51-53] fundamental optical solitons.

The symmetry-breaking instability of the ring-profile vortex solitons has been observed experimentally in both Kerrlike[54] and quadratic[55] media. In all such cases, the generation of different numbers of fundamental solitons due to the ring instability was observed. Stabilization of the ringlike vortex solitons is known to be possible only in some exceptional cases, e.g. in a special case of the competing quadratic and defocusing cubic nonlinear interaction[56]. Additionally, it was recently shown that quasi-stable propagation of optical ringlike structures carrying *integer* or *fractional angularmomentum* is possible in the formof *modulated necklace beams*[57] or *necklace-ring vector solitons*[58]. Moreover, the vectorial beam interaction was also shown to support very interesting self-trapped rotating structures in the form of 'propeller solitons'[59], that extend the conditions for the observation of stable spiralling beams.

Spatial optical solitons and soliton clusters carrying an angular momentum The main purpose of this chapter is two-fold. First of all, we briefly overview the basic physics and properties of the ring-profile solitary waves carrying a finite angular momentum and discuss a link between this type of beam selftrapped state and other ringlike structures, such as 'necklace beams'. Additionally, we demonstrate how to stabilize the expanding necklace beams by creating the so-called *soliton clusters*[60], the ringlike multi-soliton bound states with a staircase phase distribution and *nonzero angular momentum*. Secondly, we discuss the beam stabilization by incoherent coupling of several beam components, and demonstrate novel types of optical vector solitonwith rotating intensity and phase.

Scalar Vortex Solitons and Necklace-type Beams

First, we overview the fundamental physics of the scalar ringlike optical structures self-trapped in a bulk Kerr-like nonlinear medium, including the ring-profile vortex solitons and modulated necklace-type beams. These results have already been demonstrated for several types of nonlinear optical medium, including the quadratic medium, but here we consider the simplest scalar case described by the well known generalized nonlinear Schrodinger (NLS) equation, that can be derived, using the paraxial approximation, for the light propagation in an isotropic non-linear medium with a local non-linear response.

Conclusion

Solitons are truly unique entities. One of their most fascinating features is that whether the wave motion is acoustic, optical, or electrical, all solitons exhibit universal properties which transcend detailed physical mechanisms and generating equations. They exist by virtue of very strong non-linear coupling between radiation and matter.

Soliton based optical fiber communication systems, using EDFA's, are more suitable for long haul communication because of their very high information carrying capacity and repeater less transmission. These systems are still to be developed for field applications. When transmission demand will increase and device technology will improve, they will be certainly employed in field. By using soliton based optical switches multi GBPS data rate can be achieved for optical computation also.

We have presented a comprehensive overview of the recent theoretical results on the physics of the ring-profile optical solitary waves and soliton clusters carrying a finite angular momentum. Depending on the value of the total angular momentum and the cluster structure, such solitarywaves either fragment quickly into several fundamental solitons that fly off the ring, or propagate stably for many diffraction lengths with rotating intensity and phase. We have demonstrated a link between different types of ring-profile self-trapped state, such as vortex solitons, necklace beams and ringlike soliton clusters. We have also discussed the beam stabilization by incoherent coupling of several beam components, and have demonstrated the existence of novel types of ring-profile vector soliton with rotating intensity and phase. Many of these structures belong to the class of self-trapped optical beams and, therefore, they are possible only in a self-focussing optical medium. Such structures provide a nontrivial generalization to the optical vortices and phase-front dislocations, associated with the field angular momentum and spiralling optical beams.

Soliton has promised a lot of potentiality since its theory was put forward. Seven years elapsed between the discovery of optical solitons in fibers and its experimental confirmation. However, attempts for its practical implementation have been a real challenge for the soliton community for more than twenty years because of the ever-increasing demands for higher bit rate and longer distance transmission as well as the successful improvement of linear transmission quality owing to the continuous improvements in fibers and amplifiers. The potential still exists and poses a challenge to the soliton community.

REFERENCES

1. Hasegawa, A. and Y. Kodma, *Soliton in Optical Communication*, Clarendon Press, Oxford, 1995.Progress In Electromagnetics Research, PIER 74, 2007 165.
2. Iwatsuki, K., A. Takada, and M. Saruwatari, 'Observation of Optical Soliton Propagation Using GHz Gain-switched 1.3 μm Laser Diodes,' *Electron. Lett.*, Vol. 24, 1572, 1988.
3. Haus, H. and W. S. Wong, 'Soliton in Optical Communications,' *Rev. Mod. Phys.*, Vol. 68, 432–444, 1996.
4. A. Hasegawa and F. Tappert, 'Transmission of Stationary Non-linear Optical Pulses in Dispersive Dielectric Fibers. I. Anomalous Dispersion', *Appl. Phys. Lett. 23, 142 (1973).*
5. L. F. Mollenauer, R. H. Stolen, and J. P. Gordon, 'Experimental Observation of Picosecond Pulse Narrowing and Solitons in Optical fibers', *Phys. Rev. Lett. 45 (13), 1095 (1980).*
6. Haus, H. A., 'Optical Fiber Solitons: Their Properties and Uses,' *Proc. IEEE*, Vol. 81, 970–983, 1993.
7. Singh, S. P. and N. Singh, 'Non-linear Effects in Optical Fibers: Origin, Management and Applications,' *Progress In Electromagnetics Research*, PIER 73, 249–275, 2007.
8. Gardner, C S; Green, J M; Kruskal, M D and Miura, R M (1967). Method for Solving the Korteweg-de Vries Equation. Physical Review Letters 19: 1095-1097.
9. Zakharov, V E and Shabat, A B (1972). Exact Theory of Two-Dimensional Self-Focussing and One-Dimensional Self-Modulation of Waves in Non-linear Media. Soviet Physics JETP 34(1): 62-69.
10. A. Hasegawa and F. Tappert, 'Transmission of Stationary Non-linear Optical Pulses in Dispersive Dielectric Fibers. I. Anomalous dispersion', *Appl. Phys. Lett. 23, 142 (1973).*
11. J. P. Gordon, R. H. Stolen, and, L. F. Mollenauer, Phys. Rev. Lett. 45 (13), 1095 (1980).
12. Y. Silberberg and G.I. Stegeman,'One-dimensional Spatial Solitons in Kerr Media,' in: *Spatial Solitons*. S.Trillo and W.Torruellas (Springer-Verlag, Berlin, 2001), 37-60.
13. J.S.Aitchison, H.S. Eisenberg,Y. Silberberg, and R. Morandotti, Phys. Rev. Lett. **85**, 1863 (2000); See Also A.A. Sukhorukov and Yu.S. Kivshar, Phys. Rev.Lett.**87**, 083901 (2001).

14. L.du Mouza, E.Seve, H.Mardoyan, S.Wabnitz, P.Sillard, and P.Nouchi, OPt. Lett.26,1128-30(2001).

15. Yang, Y., C. Lou, H. Zhou, J. Wang, and Y. Gao, 'Simple Pulse Compression Scheme Based on Filtering Self-phase Modulation Broadened Spectrum and Its Application in an Optical time-division Multiplexing Systems,' *Appl. Opt.*, Vol. 45, 7524–7528, 2006.

16. J. H. Lee *et al.*, 'Soliton Self-frequency Shift: Experimental Demonstrations and Applications', IEEE J. Quantum Electron. 14 (3), 713 (2008).

17. V. N. Serkin and A. Hasegawa, 'Novel Soliton Solutions of the Non-linear Schrödinger Equation Model', Phys. Rev. Lett. 85 (21), 4502 (2000).

18. A. A. Voronin and A. M. Zheltikov, 'Soliton Self-frequency Shift Decelerated by Self-steepening', Opt. Lett. 33 (15), 1723 (2008)

19. Yuri S. Kivshar and Govind P. Agrawal,Optical Solitons,Elsevier Science and Technology Books, San Diego, USA, (2003).

20. Khaykovich, L (2002). Formation of a Matter-Wave Bright Soliton. Science 296(5571): 1290-1293.

21. E.A. Ostrovskaya, J.J. Garcia-Ripoll,V.M. Perez-Garcia, and Yu.S. Kivshar, Phys. Rev. Lett. **85**, 82 (2000).

22. A. Desyatnikov,D. Neshev, E. Ostrovskaya,Yu. S.Kivshar,W. Krolikowski, B. Luther-Davies, J.J. Garcia-Ripoll, and V. Perez-Garcia, Opt. Lett. **26**, 435(2001).

23. Yu.S. Kivshar and B. Luther-Davies, Phys. Rep. **298**,81 (1998).

24. A. M. Zheltikov, and A. Voronin, 'Soliton Self-frequency Shift Decelerated by Self-steepening', Opt. Lett. 33 (15), 1723 (2008).

25. X. Liu *et al.*, 'Soliton Self-frequency Shift in a Short Tapered Air–silica Microstructure Fiber', Opt. Lett. 26 (6), 358 (2001).

26. P. E. Radley, and A. W. Horsley, Proceedings of the International Conference on Submarine Telecommunication Systems, London, February 1980, pp. 173-176.

27. F. P. Kapron, Electronics Letters, Vol. 13, pp. 96-97, (1977).

28. A. Hasegawa and F. Tappert. Applied Physics Letters, Vol. 23(3), pp. 142-144, (1973).

29. L. F. Mollenauer et al, Physical Review Letters, Vol. 45(13), pp. 1095-1098, (1980).

30. S. E. Miller and A. G. Chynoweth, Editors, Academic Press, Optical Fiber Telecommunications, (1979), pp. 127-132).

31. F.Wise, X. Liu, and K. Beckwitt, Phys. Rev. Lett. **85**,1871 (2000).
32. Yu.S. Kivshar and E.A. Ostrovskaya, Opt. Photon. News **12**(4), 29 (2001).
33. J.T. Manassah, Opt. Lett. **14**, 396 (1989).
34. A.W. Snyder and F. Ladouceur, Opt. Photon. News **10**(2), 35 (1999).
35. D.N. Christodoulides, S.R. Singh, M.I. Carvalho, and M. Segev,Appl. Phys. Lett. **68**, 1763 (1996).
36. W. Krolikowski, E.A. Ostrovskaya,C.Weilnau, M.Geisser,G. McCarthy,Yu.S. Kivshar,C. Denz, and B.Luther-Davies, Phys. Rev. Lett. **85**, 1424 (2000).
37. J.D. Joannopoulos, R.D. Meade, and J.N.Winn, *Photonic Crystals: Molding the Flow of Light* (Princeton University Press, Princeton, 1995); K. Sakoda, Optical Properties of Photonic Crystals (Springer, Berlin, 2001); C.M. Soukoulis (ed.), *Photonic Crystals and Light Localization in the 21st Century* (Kluwer, Dordrecht, 2001).
38. S.F. Mingaleev and Yu.S. Kivshar, Phys. Rev. Lett. **86**,5474 (2001).
39. Ph. Ball, Nature **411**, 628 (2001).
40. M.H.Anderson *et al.*, Science **269**, 198 (1995).
41. B.P.Anderson, P.C. Haljan,C.A. Regal,D.L. Feder, L.A. Collins,C.W. Clark, and E.A. Cornell, Phys. Rev. Lett.**86**, 2926 (2001).
42. Stegeman G I and Segev M 1999 *Science* **286**,1518
43. Chiao R Y, Garmire E and Townes C H 1964 *Phys. Rev. Lett.***13** 479.
44. Haus H A 1966 *Appl. Phys. Lett.* **8** 128 Yankauskas Z K 1966 *Sov. Radiophys.* **9** 261.
45. Solja ̂ci ́cM, Sears S and Segev M 1998 *Phys. Rev. Lett.* **81** 4851 ,Solja¡ci ́c M and Segev M 2000 *Phys. Rev.* E **62** 2810.
46. Kruglov V I and Vlasov R A 1985 *Phys. Lett.* A **111** 401.
47. Kivshar Yu S and Ostrovskaya E A 2001 *Opt. Photon. News* **12**(4) 27.
48. Kruglov V I, Logvin Yu A and Volkov V M 1992 *J. Mod. Opt.* **39** 2277.
49. Atai J, Chen Y and Soto-Crespo J M 1994 *Phys. Rev.* A **49** R3170
50. Afanasjev V V 1995 *Phys. Rev.* E **52** 3153
51. Firth W J and Skryabin D V 1997 *Phys. Rev. Lett.* **79** 2450.

INDEX